Kurt Lambeck

Of Moon and Land, Ice and Strand:
Sea Level during Glacial Cycles

20 September 2013, Rome, Accademia Nazionale dei Lincei

Fondazione
Internazionale Balzan
"Premio"

Accademia Nazionale dei Lincei

Akademien der Wissenschaften Schweiz
Académies suisses des sciences
Accademie svizzere delle scienze
Academias svizras da las scienzas
Swiss Academies of Arts and Sciences

THE ANNUAL BALZAN LECTURE
5

OF MOON AND LAND, ICE AND STRAND:
Sea Level during Glacial Cycles

by
KURT LAMBECK
2012 Balzan Prizewinner

LEO S. OLSCHKI
2014

CASA EDITRICE LEO S. OLSCHKI
Viuzzo del Pozzetto, 8
50126 Firenze
www.olschki.it

ISBN 978 88 222 6339 1

CONTENTS

ALBERTO QUADRIO CURZIO

Member of the Board of the International Balzan Foundation "Prize",
President of the Class of Moral, Historical and Philological Sciences
of the Accademia Nazionale dei Lincei

FOREWORD

This Fifth Annual Balzan Lecture, delivered by Kurt Lambeck, marks another milestone for the Balzan Foundation, as the series has now established itself as a recognized element in the ongoing collaboration between the Accademia Nazionale dei Lincei, the Swiss Academies of Arts and Sciences and the Balzan Foundation to provide a platform for Balzan Prizewinners to address in public, issues and findings that are related to their Balzan Research Projects.

This series demonstrates the fundamental role of the Balzan Foundation in providing an accessible bridge between the sciences and the humanities at the highest level of international scholarship.

It gives me great pleasure to present in this occasion the fifth volume in what is a carefully crafted series of splendid contributions to contemporary academic discourse across all disciplines. In beginning this initiative we were conscious that the task would not be an easy one, but at the same time we were confident that the unparalleled caliber and capacities of the Balzan Prizewinners would ensure success. Now we have to say that the prizewinners have also contributed with enthusiasm and kindness to the initiative and also for this we are very thankful to them. Once more we have seen that great academics are also great men and women.

The first lecture in the series presented the results of research undertaken by young academics under the guidance of Peter and Rosemary Grant dealing with the seminal topic of *The Evolution of Darwin's finches, Mockingbirds and Flies.*

The second lecture by Anthony Grafton brought to life *Humanists with Inky Fingers. The Culture of Correction in Renaissance Europe* providing detailed analysis of the impact of these correctors on the meaning of the texts they were working on.

The third lecture by Colin Renfrew illustrated the findings from his excavations on the Greek island of Keros through the prism of *Cognitive Archaeology from Theory to Practice*. The series deals with subjects that have distinct contemporary relevance.

Last year Michael Marmot, with the fourth lecture, *Fair Society, Healthy Lives*, spanned the bridge between the theoretical and the practical where the empirical impinges directly on our lives in matters of life and death in his lecture.

Kurt Lambeck's lecture offers a very timely contribution not only to the debate on the consequences of human impact on the Earth, but also to the very long cycles of changes in the world's physical structure. As my very dear colleague Maria Bianca Cita Sironi says in her introduction to this Annual Balzan Lecture, Kurt Lambeck has unique scientific skills which combine Geophysics, Geology, Geodesy, Space Science, Celestial Mechanics, Environmental Geoscience and Glaciology.

From this perspective, the exposition presented in this lecture will also enable us to look at the physical and environmental phenomena from many points of view, thus avoiding the distortions of a one sided approach. Kurt Lambeck's lecture published here offers up both a distillation of research that is the fruit of decades of work and also provokes one to think in different ways about fundamental questions.

WELCOME ADDRESS BY LAMBERTO MAFFEI

President of the Accademia Nazionale dei Lincei

Distinguished Ladies and Gentlemen,

On behalf of the Accademia dei Lincei, I am very pleased to welcome you here today on the occasion of the 2013 Annual Balzan Lecture. The Lecture series, now in its fifth year, is the fruit of agreements between the International Balzan Prize Foundation, the Accademia dei Lincei and the Swiss Academies of Arts and Sciences, and aims to inform the public of scientific research in a wide range of disciplines, touching also on contemporary issues. They are delivered annually by a Balzan Prizewinner.

Today we are honoured to welcome back Professor Kurt Lambeck to deliver this year's Balzan Lecture. He is the recipient of the 2012 Balzan Prize for Solid Earth Sciences, reward for his exceptional contribution to the understanding of the relationship between sea level change and postglacial isostatic adjustment. We were fortunate to have Professor Lambeck here at the Accademia dei Lincei in November of last year, on the occasion of the Balzan Prizewinners Interdisciplinary Forum. Professor Lambeck's scientific work is distinguished by an interdisciplinary perspective to research in the field of Solid Earth Sciences. His studies have revolutionized important concepts in Solid Earth Sciences and have marked a major turning point in our understanding of climate change and its causes. Recipient of many prestigious international Prizes and member of several renowned academies, Professor Lambeck's research has been recognized worldwide.

Communication and dissemination of scientific knowledge to the public is extremely important, especially when it concerns the wellbeing of our planet. So, I thank you Professor Lambeck for accepting the invitation to deliver this year's Annual Balzan Lecture and sharing with us your observations and insight on the Earth's behaviour and geodynamic processes.

I also wish to thank the Balzan Foundation and the Swiss Academies of Arts and Sciences. The Accademia dei Lincei looks forward to many more years of fruitful collaboration.

Introduction by
ALBERTO QUADRIO CURZIO and
MARIA BIANCA CITA SIRONI Member of the Accademia Nazionale dei Lincei

Alberto Quadrio Curzio: I have the honour to convey to those present, greetings from Ambassador Bruno Bottai, President of the Balzan Foundation "Prize" who cannot be here today. He also wishes to express his appreciation to Professor Lambeck for having accepted the invitation to give this lecture. I am gratified to see that so many of you have decided to come here today, considering that there are many attractions to contend with on a Friday afternoon in early September in Rome, as "alternative experiments" incorporating sea and sand are available only a few kilometers away.

I will add a few of my own words in my capacity as Coordinator of the Balzan Joint Commission, which are involved in organizing academic endeavours with the Accademica Nazionale dei Lincei and the Swiss Academies. These endeavours include today's lecture and we are thankful to the Balzan General Prize Committee, whose duty it is to select autonomously the Balzan Prizewinners. The Balzan General Prize Committee is constituted of front rank academics and there is no better way to introduce Kurt Lambeck to cite their motivation for awarding a 2012 Balzan Prize to him: *For his exceptional contribution to the understanding of the relationship between post-glacial rebound and sea level changes. His findings have radically modified climate science.*

The format of the lecture is designed to facilitate discussion and thus following Professor Lambeck's discourse, Professors Orombelli and Doglioni will respond to the lecture and initiate an open discussion. I will now hand over to the Accademia dei Lincei's senior expert on Solid Earth Sciences, Maria Bianca Cita Sironi, who will more fully introduce Professor Lambeck and his work.

Maria Bianca Cita Sironi: I am very honoured to introduce Professor Lambeck, who is certainly a citizen of the world having worked in Australia, Europe and the US. Earlier today I asked him what was the subject of his first degree. He replied Engineering, which took me a little by surprise, because he is essentially a Geophysicist, a Geodesist, a Geologist. He started as an Engineer at a time when observations from the space had just started. These observations were very technical and recognized as very important. Thus Engineering was a useful background. Professor Lambeck has published more than 250 papers on subjects in Geophysics, Geology, Geodesy, Space Science, Celestial Mechanics, Environmental Geoscience and Glaciology, as well as two volumes on Geophysics. He remains a very active researcher, ready to take up new challenges. We look forward to listening now to what these challenges entail.

Lecture by Kurt Lambeck

OF MOON AND LAND, ICE AND STRAND:
Sea Level during Glacial Cycles

INTRODUCTION

Thank you very much for those introductory words and thank you, the audience, for giving up your afternoon on the beach on this Friday afternoon. I hope that you will find some compensation from this lecture!

I should start by explaining the title of my lecture. I am often asked why did I go into science... "what happened in your early education that steered you in that direction?" I really cannot find an answer except a book that I was given, in Dutch, when I was about eight years old. Its title was "Maan en Land, Ijs en Strand" (Moon and Land, Ice and Beach). I realized recently that the four phases in my science more or less coincide with these four subjects, although not in this order. Whether this is coincidence or not, I do not know, but I think there is one lesson: that an early exposure to science and science literature in school and in the home is an extremely important thing. This has been shown to me more recently. One of the things I have been occupied with in recent years, as President of the Australian Academy of Science, is developing programs for introducing science early in primary school education, through an approach that encourages students to ask questions about the things they see around themselves, to try and develop their own answers, and to test their hypotheses drawing on other observations and experiments. This has been a very exciting experiment indeed.

Today I am going to talk about three of the elements of my childhood book; the moon is left out other than as a cameo role. I am going to talk about the problem of the interactions between ice sheets, oceans and the solid earth: what happens when ice sheets melt; how does the earth respond; what happens to the oceans? In particular, what happens to sea level? What can we learn from this that can be relevant to other questions in geology, archaeology and pre-history?

How did I come to investigate these questions in the first place? As you have already heard from the introduction, my early career was in satellite geodesy where one of my early contributions in the late nineteen sixties was the determination of the shape of the Earth from the perturbations in satellite orbits[1]. This shape is known as the "Geoid", a gravitationally equipotential surface that contains information on the mass distribution within the planet. There is at least one person in this audience, Professor Michele Caputo, who will remember the debates about the interpretation of these gravity anomalies in the early and mid sixties. Did it mean that the earth was substantially rigid such that it could support stresses on long geological timescales? Or did it mean that the earth was dynamic; that there was convection within its interior?

My first international conference in Athens in 1965 exposed me to this conflict. One of the things I learned, and pass onto the younger generation here today is, even though I have by now become part of the old guard, listen to them but follow your own instincts. Because what soon became clear was that the satellite results provided a set of boundary conditions for the internal driving forces required to explain the then emerging plate-tectonics hypothesis.

To go from that last statement to actually modelling the dynamics of the Earth we need the viscosity of the planet's outer layers: how mantle materials behave when subjected to stress. This is controlled by its viscosity. Likewise the Earth's thermal history is controlled by the viscosity structure of the mantle. This led me to start looking at a series of geophysical problems that can be described as follows: we have an earth; it is subjected to forces; we observe its response or deformation; and ask ourselves can we infer a rheology or response function for the Earth (Fig. 1A)? Can we discover what this elastic and viscous structure of the planet is?

In geophysics there are a range of phenomena operating at different frequencies that allow us to address, in principal at least, this question

---

[1] Gaposchkin and Lambeck 1971.

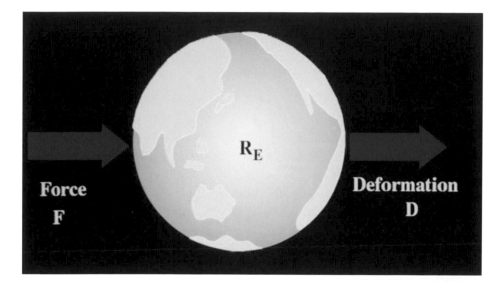

Fig. 1A. Schematic representation of the Earth's response to external or internal forcing. The Earth has a response function R_E that determines its deformation D when subjected to a force F (such as the gravitational attraction by the Moon, or an ice load on its surface). The geophysical problem is of three types: (i) knowing F and observing the D, determine R_E; (ii) knowing R_E and observing D, determine F; or (iii) a mixed problem in which improvements on both F and R_E are sought from the inversion of the observations D.

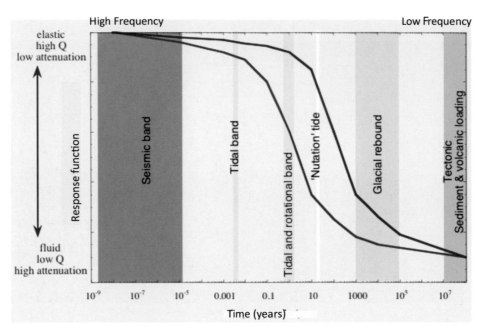

Mantle response at different forcing frequencies

Fig. 1B. A schematic representation of the Earth's response function as a function of the period (or frequency) of the deforming force. At very high frequencies (periods of the order of 1 second or less) the response of the solid Earth is essentially elastic. At very low frequencies (periods of the order >10⁷ years) the response (other than of the outer lithosphere) approaches that of a fluid. Representative frequencies of some geophysical processes that deform the Earth and yield insight into the response are shown. An important question is how does the transition from essentially elastic behaviour to essentially fluid behaviour occur. Does it follow the blue or red trajectory, or a quite different one?

of the earth's response function (Fig. 1B). At one end of the spectrum of forces we have the travel-times of seismic waves and the vibrations of the earth to infer the elastic parameters and attenuation properties in the period range from seconds to about an hour. At about 12 and 24 hours – as well as at longer periods – there are tidal deformations of the solid earth that reflect mainly an elastic response at these longer periods but an anelastic or viscous component also begins to appear. Variations in the Earth's rotation provide information at and near the annual frequency as well as at multi-decadal scales. At the other end of the spectrum, studies of tectonic processes reveal that much of the mantle acts essentially as a fluid on time scales of millions of years. The question was, and still is: how does the transition from essentially elastic behaviour to fluid behaviour occur? Is its frequency dependency something like the red spectrum in Fig. 1B, or does the transition to near-fluid behaviour occur at lower frequencies, such as the blue curve? To answer this, I started off by working my way through the spectrum, the tidal band[2] (where the moon comes into the story), the rotational band[3], and the tectonic band[4]. Lastly I turned to the glacial rebound problem[5] – the response of the earth to the waxing and waning of the ice sheets during glacial cycles – between the high-frequency tidal and rotational deformations and the tectonic part of the spectrum (Fig. 1B) and where the viscous behaviour of the mantle becomes paramount.

In all of these studies I did not achieve what I set out to do. I did not learn as much about the rheology of the Earth's mantle as I had hoped but instead learned a lot about how the other components in the earth-ocean-ice-atmosphere system respond to external and internal forcing. The Earth's response will usually reflect the combined effect of the solid and fluid regimes and, as a result, it will be contaminated by movement in the oceans, movement in the atmosphere, change in the ice sheets and by hydrological mass redistributions. So the inversion problem of Fig. 1A becomes more complex: we observed the response, or deformation; we may partially know both the mantle rheology and

---

[2] LAMBECK et al. 1974.
[3] LAMBECK 1980.
[4] STEPHENSON and LAMBECK 1985.
[5] NAKADA and LAMBECK 1987.

the forces, and from incomplete and contaminated observations we formulate the inverse model to improve our understanding about the earth's rheology as well as the fluid regimes.

GLACIAL REBOUND AND SEA LEVEL

I will illustrate some of the things I have said with what I call the "Glacial Rebound" problem. This is the question: what happens to the Earth and ocean when a large ice sheet waxes and wanes? How does the Earth and ocean respond to the changing surface load of ice and water? What observational evidence of this response can we expect? I show this in a cartoon fashion here (Fig. 2): an ice sheet that is 3-4 km thick and of 1000 km or more radius loads the lithosphere; the load stresses are propagated into the earth's interior; the stressed mantle material flows away; and the crust underneath the ice sheet subsides.

Now, this occurs in a closed – nearly incompressible – planet, so if the crust is pushed down somewhere, somewhere else it has to go up. Hence around the big ice sheet a broad zone of an uplifting crust develops and the earth's surface deformation varies from location to location and will have a characteristic time scale that is a function of the mantle viscosity. Other things also happen. When the ice sheets melt and the melt-water enters into the oceans, on average sea level rises. But the gravitational attraction between the ice and water also changes: during ice sheet growth it attracts the water so the ocean surface is not only lowered because water is removed from the ocean but the shape of its surface changes as it follows the new gravitational potential. Also, as the earth deforms under the changing ice load this gravitational potential, and hence ocean surface, is further modified.

But when ocean water is added or subtracted from the oceans and the remaining water is redistributed in response to the changing gravity field, the loads on the ocean floor are also changed and introduce additional load stresses in the lithosphere that are propagated into the mantle resulting in further mantle flow, surface deformation and change in gravitational potential. Finally, as the mass distribution and its inertia tensor of the earth-ocean-ice system is modified, so will the earth's rotation respond – as defined by the Euler equations – both in

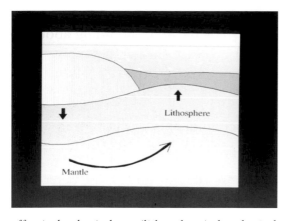

Fig. 2. Cartoon of the Earth-ocean response to the growth of an ice sheet. The sea level response consists of several components. (i) As the ice sheet grows, water is extracted from the ocean and globally averaged sea level falls. (ii) During ice sheet grows the gravitational attraction between ice and water is modified and the fall in sea level near the ice sheet margin is greater than the globally averaged fall while far from the ice sheet it is less than the global average. (iii) The load stresses are transmitted through the effectively elastic layer (lithosphere) thereby inducing convection in the mantle, and the crust beneath the ice sheet subsides. Further out from the ice margins the crust is uplifted. (iv) This mantle flow and crustal deformation further changes the gravity field and hence the ocean surface. (v) The removal and redistribution of water in the oceans changes the surface water loads to which the crust and ocean respond with additional sea level change.

terms of the rate of rotation and in the direction of the rotation axis relative to the now not-so-solid earth, modify the centrifugal force, equipotential surfaces and sea level. The conceptually simple concept quickly becomes a complex coupling of components within the ice-ocean-earth system that has to obey certain physical principles. That is, consistent with what we know about the earth's physical properties from other geophysical and laboratory measurements and an ice load that is compatible with geological and glaciological evidence. Together, these processes, which I collectively call the 'glacial isostatic effect', cause the sea level at any one time to be spatially variable and to differ from the 'eustatic' signal, or globally averaged value.

In terms of Fig. 1A, the 'force' F is the time-dependent surface load L of ice and water with the latter distributed in a gravitationally consistent way (and therefore earth-response dependent), the 'response' R is the description of the earth's rheology and includes its elastic and viscous behaviour, and the 'observations' include changes in the earth's shape and gravity, in sea level, and in rotation.

Of these observations, the most important ones are those of sea level because records are preserved in the geological record and provide evidence for the times when the last great ice sheets were disintegrating, whereas the other observations are only recorded instrumentally and 'see' only the tail end of the consequences of a deglaciation that largely ended some 8000 years ago.

If we break it down into simple components, the following would be an approximation of our mathematical model for the glacial rebound process. For the response function R: the Earth has its fluid dense core; a viscoelastic mantle whose layering and elastic behaviour we know something about from seismology but whose viscous elements η_i are unknown; and a lithosphere that is relatively cold and rigid and approximated by an effectively elastic layer of unknown thickness H. The load L is defined in the two parts of ice and water. Of the former, the ice margins are inferred from the geological record left behind by the advancing and retreating ice sheets but the record is seldom complete, particularly for the time before the Last Glacial Maximum (LGM) ~ 25,000 to 20,000 years ago. Also, direct observational estimates of the thickness of the former ice sheets are only very rarely recorded in the geological record and the mathematical description of the ice load will contain unknown ice functions I_n. The description of the water load itself requires knowledge of the ice history and of the ocean basins and how these change during the glacial cycles, with the latter provided by the glacial rebound formulation. The solution then reduces to a set of equations relating observations O of the Earth's response (with observational uncertainties ε) to the unknowns (I_n, η_I, H) through the convolution of the load L and response R functions

$$O + \varepsilon = L(I_n) \, ^* \, R(\eta_I, H)$$

The challenges are in getting the formulation of L and R correct and in having the appropriate observations that allow for a meaningful solution for the unknown parameters (I_n, η_I, H). If this can be achieved it then becomes possible to describe the behaviour of this earth-ice-ocean system under the influence of the growth and decay of ice sheets: the changing sea levels and shorelines around the world through time, quantification of the last glacial cycle, and the flow laws of mantle materials at millennium time scales.

At the start, faced with this inversion, I did what every geophysicist did; I assumed that we knew what the ice sheets were doing because we have all seen ice sheet pictures in our geography textbooks. Some of the questions we wanted to answer were: what variation in viscosity occurs with depth in the mantle? How does it vary laterally from one part of the planet to another? Is it different under the continents from under the oceans? In particular, are our linear models, assumed largely for reasons of mathematical and computational convenience, adequate? But what we quickly discovered was that the results were no better, or possibly worse, than the assumptions made about the ice sheets and that we really did not have enough a priori information about the past ice sheets. Nor did I initially appreciate the limitations of much of the observational evidence that was available and I will return to this evidence shortly. What did become clear was that a major effort would be required to extract appropriate data sets from the published literature, as well as to conduct new field investigations in critical areas. So what I thought would be a brief interlude of investigating the response spectrum in Fig. 1B at an intermediate and important frequency, quickly turned into a long-term wide-ranging and interdisciplinary research program.

But, faced with (i) incomplete data that is subject to errors and uncertainties, (ii) the occurrence of processes other than the glacial rebound contributing to sea level change, (iii) an incomplete knowledge of the ice history and (iv) overly simplified rheological models of the Earth, you may well ask the question: is it worthwhile pursuing this area of research at all? Or are we merely going around in circles?

My answer to the first part of this question is an unequivocal *yes*! It is worth doing because if we can find a satisfactory solution we can also address significant questions raised in other areas of geophysics, geology, tectonics, archaeology, pre-history, marine biology and so forth.

A HEURISTIC DESCRIPTION OF GLACIAL REBOUND AND SEA LEVEL

Fig. 3 and 4 gives some representative examples of the evidence for departures of sea level from its present position (Fig. 3) and for the quantitative interpretation of such evidence (Fig. 4) from around the world, ranging in time from the last maximum glaciation to near the present. An immediate glance shows great spatial variety in past

Fig. 3. Observational evidence indicative of the geographic variability of sea level change. (A) A raised Boulder beach from Central Sweden, formed about 9000 years ago, at ~ 200 m above present sea level. The location is south of the Ångerman River site whose sea level curve is shown in Figure 4. (B) Sea level markers on Lövgrund Island in the Baltic near Gävle (Sweden). The 'Celsius' rock, with sea level markers at 1732 (by Anders Celsius), 1832 (by Charles Lyell), 1932 (by unknown hands), points to a sea level fall of about 1m/100 years for the past 300 years. (C) Small lakes at ~ 40 m above present sea level in Andøya (northern Norway) that contain sediments deposited in marine environments. The age-height relationship of these sediments originally contributed to the sea level curve shown in Figure 4. (D) A sediment core from southern Greenland for a lake, with a similar history to that in (C), that is now isolated from the sea. The change in colour from the blue-grey marine mud to darker organic-rich sediments marks the time when the basin became isolated from the sea due to the uplift of the land (or fall in sea level relative to the land).

(E) Exposed in situ tree stumps from Borth Bog, Wales, at very low tide (www.janet-baxterphotography.co.uk). The original trees died as a result of salt contamination of groundwater due to rising sea level. Similar deposits produced the sea level curve for Exmouth, southern England, shown in Figure 4). (F) An elevated fossil coral micro-atoll, Orpheus Island, Australia, about 6000 years old that is indicative of a higher sea level 7000-6000 years ago compared to today (see Figure 4). (G) A large field of elevated micro-atolls at Kiritimati (Christmas) Island in the Pacific indicating that here sea levels have been nearly constant for the past 5000 years. (H) Coring into sediments from a frozen lake in Vestfold Hills, Antarctica, yielding evidence for falling sea level along the East Antarctic coast during the past 8000 years.

sea level from one location to another, a variation that can also be expected for recent sea level change and in a first approximation can be understood as the combination of the Earth's crustal deformation in response to the deglaciation and the increase in ocean volume.

In the Gulf of Bothnia between Sweden and Finland, there are boulder beaches that formed at a time when the ice margin stood at the shoreline (Fig. 3A). These, along with other shoreline indicators, now occur up to 200 meters and more above sea level, with the higher ones dating from about 9000 years ago and followed by a nearly exponential fall up to the present (Fig. 4A), a process that is still on-going today at a rate of nearly 1 cm/year (Fig. 3B). Here the crustal uplift, following the removal of some 2500-3000 m of ice, completely dominates the sea level rise occurring from the melt water added into the oceans during the global deglaciation phase (I will refer to this loosely as the eustatic component) (Fig. 5A). Such observations provide some constraint on the amount of ice previously over the locality, as well as on the time constants of the mantle response. Similar variations in sea level change are seen around the Hudson Bay of Canada. Not that far away from Bothnia, in Norway on the island of Andøya, we see a different behaviour, with an initially falling sea level, then rising, and then falling again (Fig. 4B). The observations here are from the discovery of marine sediments in small lakes that became isolated from the sea as the land was uplifted and that are now up to about 40 meters above sea level (Fig. 3C). Here, the crustal rebound is smaller because the site is near the edge of the former ice sheet. Initially this rebound dominates over the eustatic component but at a later stage the two are equal and of opposite sign. This is followed by a period up to the end of the deglaciation when the eustatic component – primarily from the much larger North American ice sheet – dominates. Finally the remnant relaxation of the mantle takes over such that sea levels locally are falling relative to the crust (Fig. 5B). This curve therefore tells us when the bulk of the melting stopped, something about the relaxation times of the mantle, and something about the ice thickness before the area became ice-free. Similar sea level curves are seen in southern Greenland, Scotland, the Maritime Provinces of Canada, and, importantly, East Antarctica.

Further from the ice sheets again, such as in southern England, the French Atlantic coast, or the southeast coast of the USA and across the

Caribbean, the eustatic component becomes the dominant contribution but the crustal rebound remains significant. In this case the latter is one of subsidence as the broad deformational-gravitational bulge that formed around the ice sheet during the loading phase, relaxes and subsides. Hence the total sea level is initially one of rapid rise while the eustatic component dominates followed by a more gradual rise during the post-glacial period (Fig. 5C). Evidence for this latter period is often found as remnants of submerged forests or pre-historic landmarks (Fig. 3E). Such curves therefore provide insight into the amount and timing of the addition of melt water – of the total amount of ice added – and, from the post-glacial part of the record, information on the relaxation process.

Far from the former ice sheets, along continental coast lines or at mid-ocean islands, sea levels at ~ 22,000 years ago were at -110 to -130 m meters, depending on locality, initially rising slowly then rapidly until about 7000 years ago (see the Barbados and Sunda Shelf results, Fig. 4E,F). Such observations provide essentially information on the eustatic change but their variability from site to site also tells us something about the mantle response function. At such sites, small-amplitude highstands in sea level, ~ 6000 years old, are often seen (Fig. 3F,G), for example as fossil corals above their present growth limits. This is mainly a consequence of the melt water loading the ocean floor and the crust subsiding, partially dragging the coastal zones down with it. This continues after the ice volumes have stabilized and coastal sea level will fall slowly. Hence the earlier period of sea level rise changes to a time of sea level fall during the postglacial phase, leaving the highstands (Fig. 5D). These corals can be particularly important when they form 'micro-atolls' whose morphology indicates that they grew up to the mean-low-water-spring tide level. Where they are abundant they can provide a near continuous record of sea level change, as for Christmas Island in the Pacific Ocean (Fig. 3G). At this latter site the various isostatic and eustatic factors come together so as to nearly cancel out and here we have clear evidence that sea level oscillations on a multi-centennial time scales have not exceeded about 25 cm for the few millennia before ~ 1900 AD (Fig. 4H).

This tell-tale pattern of global sea level is what allows us to separate the earth and ice contributions to sea level change. Whether the data is from the centre or margin of the former glaciation, or whether it is far

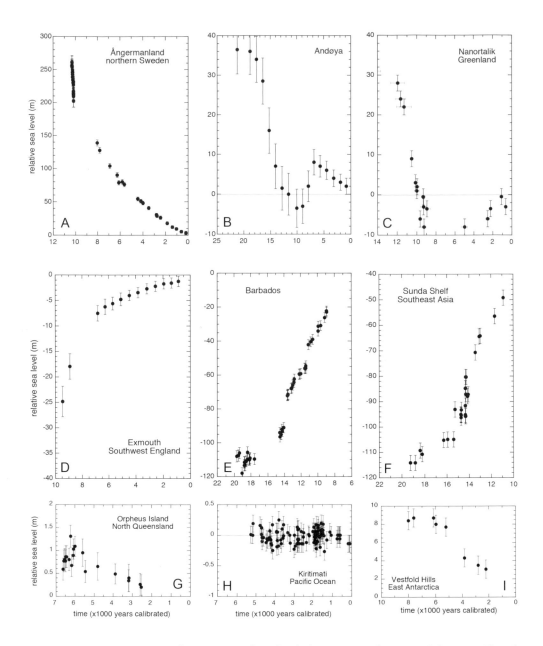

Fig. 4. Representative observations of sea level change since the time of the Last Glacial Maximum from globally distributed areas that are free of tectonic movements or where it has been possible to predict vertical land movement of tectonic cause (as in the case of Barbados). Note the difference in time and elevation/depth scales for the different locations. (A) Ångerman River (northern Sweden); (B) Andøya (northern Norway); (C) Nanortalik, southern Greenland; (D) Exmouth, southwest England; (E) Barbados; (F) Sunda Shelf and South China Sea; (G) Orpheus Island, Australia; (H) Kiritimati Island, Pacific Ocean; (I) Vestfold Hills, East Antarctica.

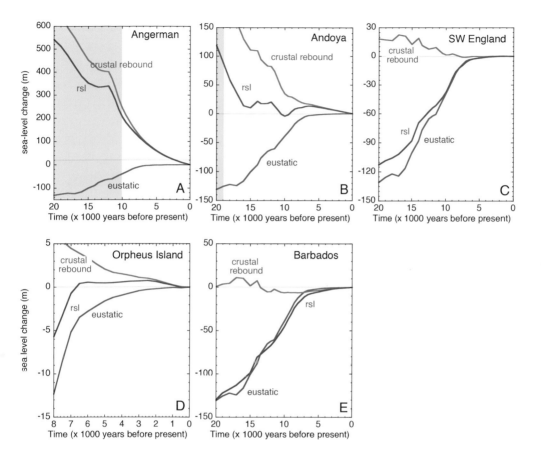

Fig. 5. Schematic illustrations of the principal components of relative sea level change. (A) Sites within the former margins of large ice sheets (e.g. Ångerman River, Fig. 4). (B) Sites near the margins of former ice sheets (e.g. Andøya, Vestfold Hills, Fig. 4). (C) For locations outside of the former ice sheets and on the broad peripheral bulge that develops there (see Fig. 2)(e.g. Exmouth, southwest England). (D) For continental margin sites far from the former ice sheets (e.g. Orpheus Island, Australia). (E) For an ocean island site (Barbados). The blue curves represent the spatially independent eustatic component and the green curves represent the spatially variable isostatic component, including the crustal response to the ice-water load and gravitational effects. The brown curves represent the position of sea level at a time in the past relative to the present (t=0). The blue zones in A and B identify the times at which the site would have been ice covered. Note the different time and sea level change scales for the five panels.

from these centres, each part of the sea level curve tells us something about the ice sheets and about the Earth's response function.

IN SEARCH OF OBSERVATIONAL EVIDENCE

As already mentioned, the most complete record of evidence for sea level change is from the geological record: in the form of raised or submerged palaeo shorelines, expressed as wave-cut platforms or erosion notches, as tidal sediment deposits, or as in situ submerged tree roots or emerged corals and bivalves (Fig. 3). The measurement is one of the age and elevation of the fossil sea level indicator relative to its present-day equivalent and represents a change in the ocean height relative to the land. An elevated shoreline indicates either that sea level has fallen because of a reduction in ocean volume – and hence, on the glacial time scale, an increase in grounded ice – or that the land has moved up. In most cases it will be a combination of the two: the glacial rebound producing both ocean volume and land movement changes, and other, so far unspoken off tectonic land movements. We refer to this measure, therefore, as relative sea level. Issues that must be assessed about such observations include: Is the formation position of the sea level indicator known? Salt marsh deposits usually form at the upper part of the tidal range, but has the tidal range changed since their formation at this location? Corals, depending on species, can grow up to a well-defined low tide level, but at what depth did the in situ fossil sample actually live? Are the bivalves in situ or have they been wind-blown up the shoreline or sunk post-death to a depth below their normal habitat? Where was the saline water table relative to mean sea level at the time that the now-drowned forest died? Have the sediments within which the markers occur been compacted under subsequent sediment loading or because of dewatering? Are the ages of growth or formation of the sea level markers accurately preserved in an 'absolute' time frame? Is the published sea level curve a composite of observations from different locations between which spatial variability can be expected because of the glacio-isostatic effects such that it has to be de-constructed? And so forth.

So in developing the geophysical models we have to remind ourselves that the observations are themselves the result of geological model assumptions and we have to ask ourselves each time: are the fundamental assumptions made in obtaining these observations valid or not? Fortunately over a period of decades, Quaternary geologists have become increasingly aware of these issues such that the data quality is only improving with time.

Archaeological evidence for past sea levels often comes in the form of limiting values. Submerged sites of early settlement indicate that sea levels at the time of human activity must have been below the site but the unknown often is by how much? In some special cases we can be more specific. One example is provided by coastal wells in Caesarea, Israel, whose use were transformed from a source of fresh-water to a rubbish bin once rising sea levels contaminated the groundwater.[6] A more precise indicator is provided by Roman-epoch fish tanks, constructed between about 100 BC and 100 AD. Here the combination of precise hydraulic requirements for regulating flow into and out of the tanks with small amplitudes of the Mediterranean tides has provided an effective tide gauge from 2000 years ago[7].

What we have done over a period of time is to collect data, either from published sources or from our own field experiments from critical areas, for different parts of the world to address different aspects of the overall solution or for particular geophysical, geological or archaeological applications. Fig 6 shows some of the areas where we have worked in the past, with the red areas being ones that have been or are being supported in part by the International Balzan Prize Foundation. I will touch on some of those projects later.

ANALYSIS APPROACH

A few words on how our analysis of the glacial rebound problem has evolved over time may be appropriate to illustrate how we try to separate out some of the unknowns. We started off with (i) a preliminary ice model that produces a time-dependent function of the globally integrated changes in ice volume $\Delta V_{ice}(t)$, (ii) with an initial parameterized function E of the Earth's rheology, and (iii) a

---

[6] SIVAN et al. 2001.
[7] CAPUTO & PIERI 1972; LAMBECK et al. 2004a.

set of published observations. Then, following the global pattern of the observations as illustrated in Figures 3 and 4, we separated the analysis into two parts. The first is the 'far-field' analysis of data far from the former ice margins where the sea level signal is determined mainly by $\Delta V_{ice}(t)$ and is insensitive to how the ice was distributed between the various ice sheets.

The first inversions of the far-field data set yielded improved estimates of these two functions $\Delta V_{ice}(t)$ and E_o, with E_o denoting ocean mantle response since the principal isostatic signal at the far-field continental margin locations is from the change in water loading. The second group of observations are from the 'near-field', within or close to the former ice margins where the response is sensitive to the details of the changes in the former ice sheets. These inversions provide corrections to the model of the particular ice sheet being analysed $\delta V_{ice}(t,\varphi)$ (φ indicating a spatial dependence of the ice distribution in addition to the time dependence) as well as estimates of the predominantly continental mantle E_c beneath the ice sheets. Inversions are then carried out for each subgroup of data corresponding to the major ice sheets of the northern hemisphere, starting with the smallest (that over Britain) and working towards the largest (North America), on the bases that the response to small ice sheets is primarily a function of the upper mantle viscosity and the response to large ice sheets is also sensitive to lower mantle rheology.

At the end of the first iteration of far-field and near-field analyses, we test the condition that

$$\sum_n \delta V_{ice}^n(t,\varphi) = \Delta V_{ice}(t)$$

where the summation is over the number of ice sheets analysed. Any discrepancy in this condition then leads to a search to where the ice missing from (or in excess of) the summation can be located or where the local solutions need to be improved through introducing better observational constraints. The initial inference was that much of this 'missing ice' had to originate from Antarctica (whose earlier glacial history is not well known) and this becomes the hypothesis to be tested.

In the second iteration of solutions, armed with the improved ice sheet models and after a redistribution of the 'missing ice' we returned to the far-field analysis, with improved observational data, and repeated first the far-field solution and then the near-field solutions and repeating the entire process until convergence occurs. Once reasonably convergence was achieved we then turned our attention to the earlier part of the glacial cycle.

The analyses of the individual ice sheets are largely limited to the last deglaciation because records of earlier phases of ice sheet growth and decay have been largely destroyed by the most recent ice history. But this earlier period is important for at least two reasons. One is that the analyses for the last phase of the glacial cycle are dependent on some knowledge of the ice history leading up to the maximum glaciation. The other is that this earlier period is important for understanding conditions at the time of onset of glaciation and for developing an improved understanding of the response of ice sheets and sea level to changes in climate during interglacial conditions such as that of today. Thus armed with what we have learned about the earth-ice-ocean interactions for the past 20,000 or so years, and as part of our iterative process, we use the increasingly sparse data to extend the analyses further back in time: to the penultimate glacial maximum so as to include the last interglacial period (~ 130,000 to 120,000 years ago) that provides an important guide to the possible future behaviour of sea level in recent millennia.[8]

SOME RESULTS: PAST AND RECENT

Global sea level and ice volume

The most recent iteration of the far-field analysis is illustrated in Fig. 7 and has involved two young researchers, Héléne Rouby from Paris and Yiying Sun from Hong Kong, both partially supported from the Balzan funds. They have put together new data sets for the sea level change for the last 35,000 years from the Indian Ocean and the eastern and south-eastern coast of Asia and in so doing have considerably expanded our far-field data base. This is leading to a much-improved assessment of both the ice-volume function $\Delta V_{ice}(t)$ and the mantle viscosity for ocean environments.

---

[8] LAMBECK et al. 2006, 2010a. DUTTON and LAMBECK 2012.

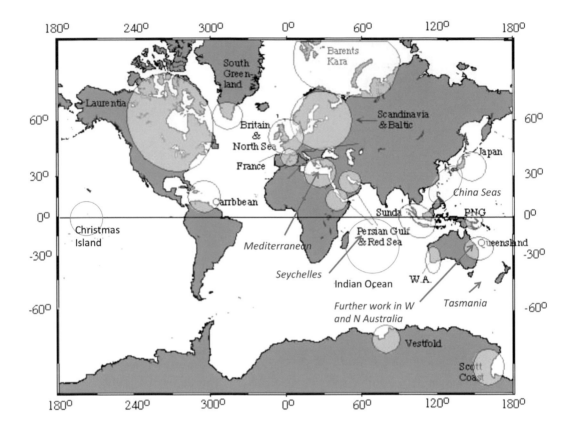

Fig. 6. Locations where we have carried out analyses of sea level change, including our own field work, and areas (in red) where Balzan students/fellows are currently working or where projects are under discussion.

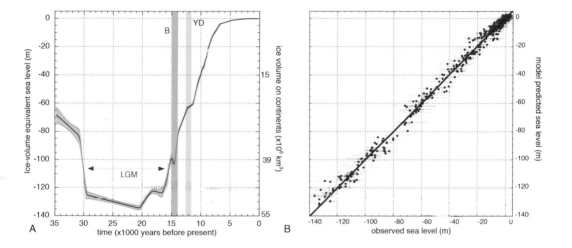

Fig. 7. (A) A new solution for the change in global mean sea level and ice volume for the past 35,000 years. B refers to a relatively warm interval, the Bølling period, during which ice melted rapidly to produce a globally averaged sea level rise of ~ 20m in less than 500 years, at a rate >40mm/year. YD refers to the short-duration cold period known as the Younger Dryas. At the last time of maximum glaciation (LGM) some 50-55 million km³ more ice was stored on the continents and grounded on the continental shelves than today. (B) a comparison of observed sea levels and model-predicted values for the same period. The high correlation (99%) between the two indicates that we have an effective model for predicting sea levels and shoreline locations for sites far from the former ice margins.

What we see is that globally the ice sheets contained some 52 million cubic kilometers more ice on the continents and grounded on the shelves than today. When this was added to the oceans, starting at about 20,000 years ago, it raised globally averaged sea level, the eustatic sea level introduced earlier, by some 135 m over ~ 13,000 years at a long-term average rate of ~ 10 mm/year. Periods of particularly rapid addition of melt water around 14,500 years ago are quite clearly identified in this global compilation (corresponding to the Bølling interstadial interval when temperatures in the northern hemisphere were relatively – compared to the earlier glacial conditions – warm) with a eustatic rise of ~ 20 m in about 500 years (~ 40mm/year). At about 12,500 years for a duration of 500 years the rise slowed down and sea levels may even have stabilised for this short time interval, corresponding to the Younger Dryas cold period in which the northern hemisphere again approached near glacial conditions. By ~ 7000 years ago the melting had largely ceased and eustatic sea level stabilized (but not local sea levels) and ocean volumes increased only slowly thereafter, at ~ 0.5 mm/year, until before about 2500 years ago.

With this solution for $\Delta V_{ice}(t)$ and the earth parameters E_o we can predict local and regional sea levels in the far-field for the past 20,000 years and compare this with the observational evidence, as is done in Figure 7B. Agreement is within both observational and model uncertainties and this suggests that we have a very effective interpolator of the spatial- and time-variable sea level for areas far from the former ice sheets and that is relatively independent of how the ice was distributed between the ice sheets. Hence we can use such models with a high degree of confidence to reconstruct palaeo shorelines and bathymetries in areas such as the Persian Gulf, the Red Sea, and Bass Strait between the Australian continent and Tasmania, to examine possible land bridges and migration routes (Fig. 8). Early migration into Sumer from the east could, for example, have occurred along an evolving Euphrates river-lake-swamp system (Fig. 8A) that flowed into the Indian Ocean at Hormuz until about 7000-6000 years ago when sea levels peaked a meter or two above its current level and flooded the Euphrates Delta and the Hammar Lakes as far as the Sumerian sites of Obeid, Ur and Eridu[9]. More recently, it has been possible to

---

[9] LAMBECK 1996.

reconstruct the topography and bathymetry at the southern end of the Red Sea (Fig. 8B) and examine the conditions for crossing the residual waterway at times of sea level lowstands going as far back as ~ 400,000 years.[10] One of the things that we are currently examining are the tidal conditions through the very much-restricted Bab-el-Mandeb at glacial times and whether these would have hampered human movements out of Africa into the Arabian Peninsula as suggested by some archaeological evidence. In the Australian example, the reconstructions identify windows of opportunity for early settlement of Tasmania as well as the timing of long intervals of isolation.[11] We have not yet revisited these questions using our most recent and higher resolution solutions but this is something that we will endeavour to do with the Balzan funding.

On Ice Sheets

Fennoscandinavia, with a long record of careful studies of the landscape evolution since the last glaciation, is a key area for developing and testing the rebound models and using the sea level data to constrain models of the ice sheets. Fig. 9 illustrates some representative examples of observations of sea level across this region and these can be readily understood from the schematic illustrations in Fig. 5. The Ångerman River observations we have already seen and point to this location being near the center of the former ice sheet. The Andøya result, likewise, we have seen and is representative of many locations along the Norway coast except that the area here was ice-free much earlier than further south (see the Bugn, Sør Trøndelag, result). In south western Norway almost no change in sea level occurred for over a period of 16,000 years indicating that the isostatic and eustatic components tended to balance out throughout this period and that there could not have been thick ice over the North Sea to merge with the Scottish ice. In the Oslo Graben there appears to have been a rapidly falling sea level after the area became ice-free following the Younger Dryas cold period, suggesting rapid retreat of initially thick ice. In the Danish Bælt region observed Late-Glacial sea levels never rose above present pointing to the ice cover over that area having

---

[10] LAMBECK et al. 2011.
[11] LAMBECK and CHAPPELL 2001.

been relatively thin, probably less than about 300 m. So even from a rather casual examination of the field date it becomes possible to infer properties of the former ice sheet.

Over a period of several years we were able to put together a large database of some 3200 observations with each point providing a relationship between land and ocean surface movements or between ice thickness and mantle rheology. From the inversion of this database, coupled with an interpretation of the field data pertaining to the ice movements back and forth across the region, we have been able to develop a quite comprehensive model of the evolution of this ice sheet from the time of the onset of the last full glacial cycle starting at about 120,000 years ago. I show just three epochs here (Fig. 10). The first, for ~ 28,000 years ago, is leading into the Glacial Maximum with ice reaching its maximum extent across the North Sea while a large part of Finland and south of the Baltic was still largely ice-free. By 21,000 years the ice sheet has grown east and southwards, but at the same time thinning over the Gulf of Bothnia, which is suggestive of a collapse of the central ice dome, reaching its maximum limits across Denmark and the North German Plain. By the third epoch, corresponding to the Younger Dryas at 12,500 years ago, a significant retreat had occurred leaving a large lake, the Baltic Ice Lake, at some 25 m above the sea level and overflowing through the Danish Bælts. Fig. 11, comparing

Fig. 8. Palaeogeographic reconstructions for three locations. (A,B) The Persian Gulf at 15,000 and 12,000 years ago respectively. At the former epoch the level of the Indian Ocean is below the sill of Hormuz and a large freshwater lake/swamp system develops in the lower part of the Gulf. Shortly after, global sea level has risen above the sill and the first marine incursion into the Gulf occurs. The Gulf floor provides a gently sloping terrain, in contrast to the rugged terrain immediately to the north, on both sides of the river system, similar to the more recent landscape of the Hammar Lakes, and a rather obvious migration route out of India into Mesopotamia. (C,D) The southern end of the Red Sea at 20,000 and 12,000 years ago. At the former period the entrance to the Red Sea is defined by a long and narrow channel that bifurcates into a series of shallow channels at the latitude of the Hanish Islands. The maximum crossing distance between Africa and Arabia via the then-existing islands is only a few km with intervisibility of both shores at all times. Even at 12,000 years ago the channels remain narrow. (E,F) Bass Strait between the Australian continent and Tasmania at 18,000 and 14,000 years ago. During the glacial period most of the Strait was above sea level with a central shallow basin fed by north-flowing rivers from Tasmania. By 14,000 years ago the land-bridge had become tenuous. Short-duration connections may have existed between the end of the last interglacial and the onset of the last glacial maximum.

Persian Gulf
T = 15 000 years BP

A

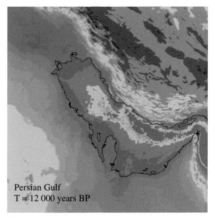

Persian Gulf
T = 12 000 years BP

B

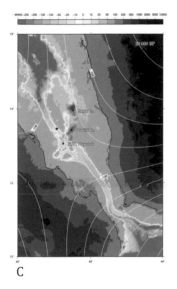

C

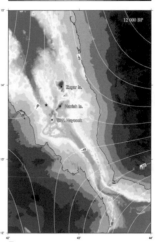

D

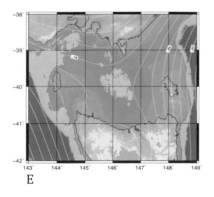

E

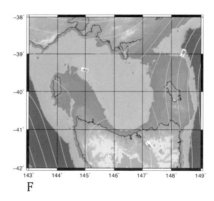

F

model predictions with the observations, indicates a high degree of agreement and that here also we have a reliable predictive model for sea level and shoreline migrations through time.

Less deterministic is the solution for the North American ice sheet for which there is a much less satisfactory observational database. Nevertheless we have been able to make some progress. The classical picture of this ice sheet is of a large single dome centered over the Hudson Bay. Instead our inversions indicate that the ice sheet is more likely to have consisted of multiple domes with one to the west of the Hudson Bay, another, smaller one, to the south, a third over Quebec Province, and further ones over the Arctic islands of Canada. There is still work to be done on improving this model with Balzan Fellow Anthony Purcell.

Of greater uncertainty are the changes in Antarctic ice volume since the time of maximum glaciation, in large part because there are few ice-free areas where records of ice retreat can be observed. But when we compare the most-recent estimates of ice volumes from our regional solutions with the total change in ice volume inferred from the global solution, we find a substantial difference, equivalent to ~ 20-25 m of global sea level change. We can only explain this in terms of the Antarctic ice sheet having been significantly larger during the last glacial maximum and we distribute the 'missing' ice, into Antarctica, guiding our distribution by locations of offshore moraines and simple glaciological models. Unless you are a glaciologist, it may not seem a surprising result that this ice sheet was significantly larger in the past but the limited available field evidence does not appear to support this. We were aware of this inference already in 1988 and one of the first things we did was to seek new information on crustal rebound along the Antarctic margin, from sediments collected in small lakes that were once in contact with the sea[12], similar to the basins of northern Norway (see Fig. 3). This did lead to the inference that substantial reduction in ice did occur in this area of the Vestfold Hills. But can this be extrapolated to much of the rest of East Antarctica, as is required to explain the above 20-25 m of missing ice? So another test is to examine areas beyond Antarctica that should

---

[12] ZWARTZ et al. 1998.

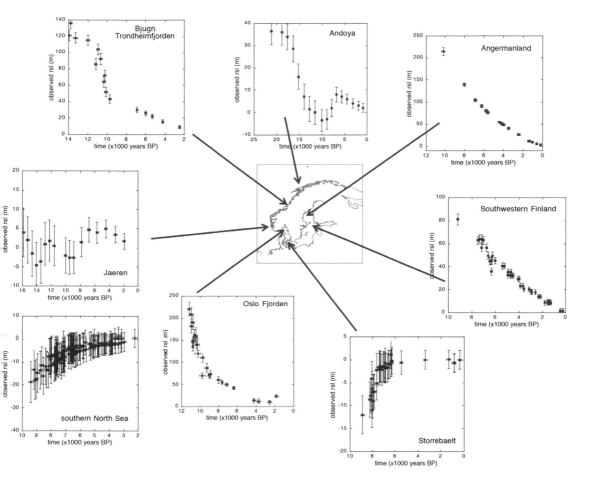

Fig. 9. Representative observations of sea level change across Fennoscandinavia and northern Europe.

be subsiding if there had been a substantially larger Antarctic ice sheet. Opportunities for this are few because many of the far southern shores occur in tectonically active areas or are not conducive to the precise preservation of shoreline information. But locations have recently been found in Tasmania and, with the assistance of Balzan funding for Brigid Morrison from the University of Tasmania, we have identified crustal subsidence that appears to be consistent with our Antarctic ice models. This is still an on-going project and we plan to collect further data during 2014.

Mantle rheology

We have described our earth response functions with what are little more than zero-order approximations of the behaviour of real earth materials. Hence they must be considered as 'effective' parameters that describe an integrated response over length scales comparable to the scale of the ice sheets and oceans and over time scales commensurate with those of the unloading cycle. Nevertheless, some useful indicators are beginning to emerge. One is the depth dependence of the 'effective' Newtonian mantle viscosity, with an increase in value of ~ 20-100 between the depth averaged upper and lower mantle values. The other is evidence for lateral variation in effective viscosity of the upper mantle from low values near 10^{20} Pa s beneath oceans and ~ 5×10^{20} beneath the North American continent. How these inferences may relate to the behaviour observed in the laboratory presents some challenges but the fact that the patterns observed are consistent with evidence from seismic-wave attenuation experiments, for example, is encouraging. One of the things that we will be doing through Balzan funding is explore alternative formulations of the rheology.

Sea levels in the Mediterranean

In working in the Mediterranean I have enjoyed the support of many researchers in geology, geodesy and archaeology, most notably in Italy from Drs Fabrizio Antonioli from ENEA[13] and Marco An-

---

[13] Agenzia nazionale per le nuove tecnologie, l'energia e lo sviluppo economico sostenibile, Rome.

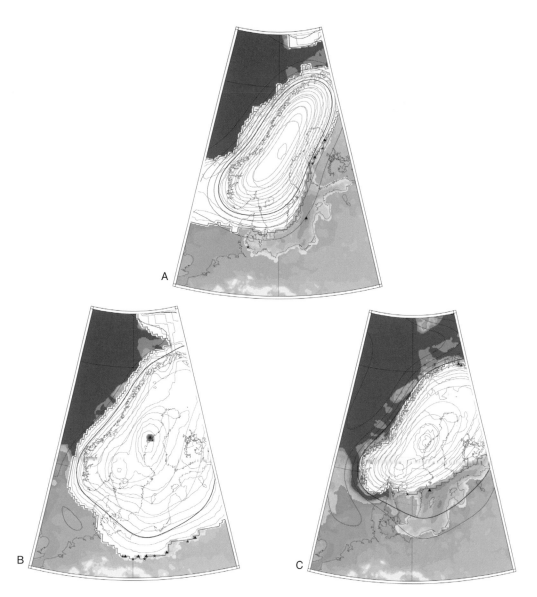

Fig. 10. Ice sheet reconstructions for Scandinavia at three epochs during the last glaciation. (A) At 28,000 years ago, corresponding approximately to the global onset of maximum glaciation and to the maximum advance of the Scandinavian ice onto the Norway Self and North Sea. (B) At 21,000 years ago when the ice has reached its maximum limits over Denmark and northern Germany, but not yet in the east. (C) At 12,500 years ago, a cold period known as the Younger Dryas, when the Baltic formed a freshwater lake about 25 m above coeval sea level, draining out across the Oresund and Danish Bælts. Ice-thickness contours (blue) are 200 m. The positive relative sea level contours (indicating the local change in sea level from the epoch to present) are indicated in orange, and negative contours in red, with contour intervals of 40 m for 28,000 year, 150 m for 21,000 year, and 30 m for 12,500 years ago.

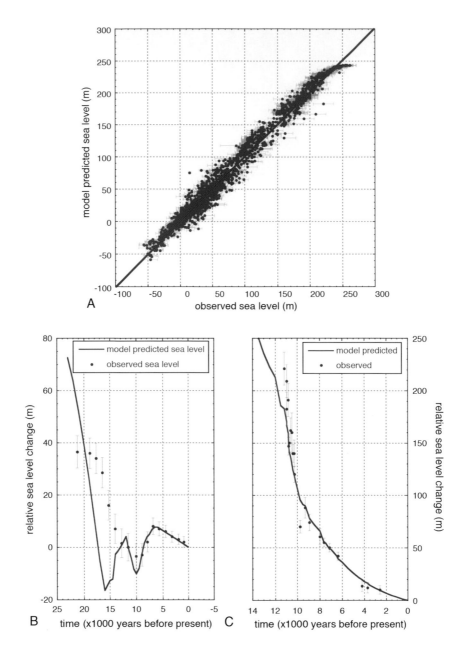

Fig. 11. (A) Comparison of model predictions with observed values across Fennoscandinavia and northern Europe. The high correlation (>99%) between the two indicates that the ice-earth model parameters are effective for predicting sea levels and shoreline locations for sites across this region. Some significant discrepancies between the two occur pointing to inadequacies in the ice model over the Andøya near the time of maximum glaciation (B) or over the Oslo Graben (C) where the very rapid fall in sea level observed at around 11,000 years ago is predicted to occur earlier.

zidei from INGV[14] and their colleagues. We have learnt a lot about regional geology, sea level and coastal archaeology but much can still be done so what I say here should only be seen as an interim report. The Mediterranean is a region where sea level has been and continues to be under the influence of the deglaciation of the two great northern hemisphere ice sheets over northern Europe and North America. As a result, it is mostly a region of rising sea level from the time of the onset of deglaciation up to the present as mantle materials flow towards the region beneath the decaying ice sheets (similar to Figs. 4D, 5C). At the same time the water load within the Mediterranean has increased by some 135 m, depressing the sea floor and adjacent margins regionally by amounts that are a function of the distribution of this water load. This is illustrated in Fig. 12A for 20,000 years ago. Combined, these two contributions result in a regional variation in LGM sea levels from about 100 m to 135 m below present, with associated strong gradients in the load stresses in the lithosphere and crust across the continental margins. The question could be asked whether these additional stresses modulate in some way the tectonic stress state such that we can expect a causal relation between past sea level rise and seismicity.

The pattern illustrated in Fig. 12A is predicted, but with time-dependent amplitudes, for the next 20,000 years up to the present. Geological evidence for sea level change abounds around the shores of the Mediterranean (Fig. 13) but testing of this model is difficult because it is also a region of active tectonics driven by the convergence of the African and Eurasian tectonic plates. Within this region of geological turmoil there are areas of quiescence identified by low levels of seismic activity and by shorelines of last interglacial age that lie within a few meters of present-day sea level. Thus we have a basis for developing predictive models for sea level across the region: we (i) develop our isostatic models; (ii) test them outside the Mediterranean region for general validity; (iii) identify the more stable parts within the Mediterranean to test the validity of the models there and fine tune the regional earth-model parameters if required; (iv) predict the isostatic-eustatic change and compare this with observations of

---

[14] Istituto Nazionale di Geofisica e Vulcanologia, Rome.

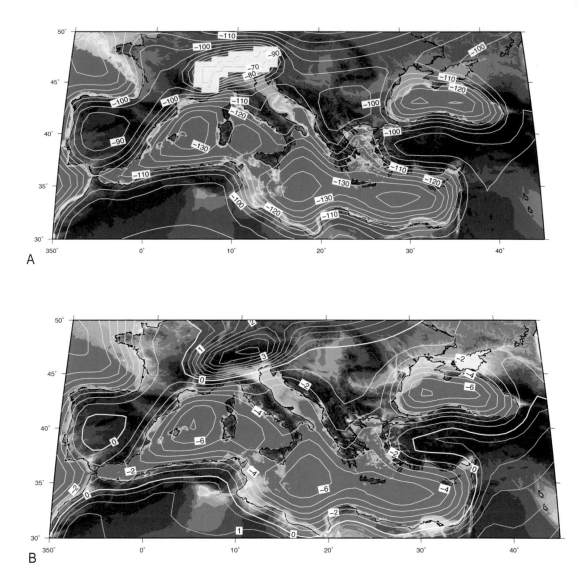

Fig. 12. Mediterranean sea level reconstructions at (A) the Last Glacial Maximum, and (B) at 6000 years ago. The contours represent the position of palaeo sea level with respect to present. In (A) exposed areas at 20,000 years ago are in the pale brown shades. Much of the northern Adriatic is exposed at this time with a nearly enclosed shallow lagoon in its central part. Sediment cores from this location could be important for testing the model. Note the land bridge to Malta and the closure of the Messina Strait. The Black Sea is isolated from the Mediterranean at this time and for a substantial time thereafter.

past sea levels for the tectonically active areas and estimate rates of tectonic uplift and subsidence; (v) combine the isostatic and tectonic contributions to predict rates of future change due to this combined geological signal to provide the background signal upon which recent contributions of anthropogenic cause are superimposed[15].

Geological and archaeological data from the more stable regions and for the Holocene period largely support the eustatic-isostatic models developed to date[16] but additional information is desirable for the earlier period. One area worth examining further is in the central Adriatic where a shallow-water basin is predicted during the LGM, sediments from which could provide a good test of the early part of this model. If anyone in the audience has access to such material I would appreciate hearing about it.

The predicted sea level change 6000 years ago assuming tectonic stability is illustrated in Fig. 12B. The mid-Holocene highstands well developed further from the former ice sheets (as in Fig. 3G) are not seen here (with possible one or two exceptions, in the southeast corner of the Mediterranean and in the Gulf of Gabès in Tunisia) and sea levels have continued to rise to the present. One example of this is shown in Fig. 14, as the comparison of observations with model predictions for the Tiber Plain[17]. The former are of three types: upper limits to past sea level, in the form of terrestrial material that was deposited above sea level; lower limits consisting of marine organisms that live in shallow marine waters; and 'transitional' deposits from the inter-tidal zone. Hence the actual sea level curve must lie between the two limiting types of observations and through the transitional ones, very much as the model prediction. While the challenge is to test these models further, we do appear to have a reasonably effective predictive model for at least the isostatic contributions to sea level. Any new observations are most welcome!

Despite room for improvement (could do better, I hear one of my teachers say long ago!), I consider that we have a good first-order predictive model for the background sea level change during an important period of early human movements and coastal settlements,

---

[15] Lambeck et al. 2010b.
[16] Lambeck et al. 2004b.
[17] Lambeck et al. 2010c.

as well as for looking at future change. But I will first digress to an earlier period in geological time for which our models may also be relevant. This is time of the Messinian Salinity Crisis[18], about 5.5 million years ago when the Strait of Gibraltar was closed by the tectonic convergence of Africa and Europe. This resulted in an enclosed sea that became desiccated through evaporation of more than 2000 m of water or about 15 times the magnitude of the glacial melt water loading. The Earth's response to this unloading would have been similar in pattern to that illustrated in Fig. 12A, but scaled upwards, with a differential sea-floor rebound across the basin of about 600 m. With deviatoric stresses in the lithosphere reaching several MPa, major failure may have occurred in the crust around the entire basin. This calculation, to my knowledge, has not been done in detail but the tools are there to do it using the well-tested glacial isostatic formulation.

Returning to the more recent period of Fig. 12A, what we also see are much expanded continental shelves leading to land bridges between some of the present islands. For Italy these occur between Calabria and Sicily; between Corsica and Sardinia with a sea crossing between Italy and Corsica reduced to the separation between I. di Capraia and Cap Corse; and between Sicily and Malta with the separation of the latter from North Africa reduced but still some 60 km wide. This raises the question whether evidence for the migration of fauna and flora across the region and between the islands has been missed because the then favourable coastal routes are now submerged and beyond ready scrutiny?

Any discussion of past migration routes is of course compounded by tectonic considerations. For example, the timing and duration of the Calabria-Sicily land bridge will be a function of the tectonics of the region, but using the strategy outlined above, of identifying where vertical tectonics is likely to be important and correcting for it using independent estimates, it is possible to develop realistic scenarios of the evolution of this land bridge, including of the tidal and other environmental conditions, as reported a few days ago in Il Messaggero.[19]

I earlier mentioned the Roman epoch fish tanks which, in order to function effectively, must bear a very sharply defined relation to

---

[18] Hsü et al. 1973.
[19] 17 September 2013.

Fig. 13. Examples of observational evidence for local relative sea level change across the Mediterranean. A. Three raised marine terraces from Lamezia Terme, Calabria, at elevations of ~ 150, ~ 400 and ~ 600 m above present sea level, probably corresponding to successive interglacials. This area is characterized by long-term land uplift. B. Sea caves in Gibraltar at present sea level and at three distinct higher levels corresponding to successive interglacials and pointing to systematic, long-term tectonic uplift of the coast (Photo G. Bailey). C. Erosion notch, about 7-8 m high observed along the cliffs of the Gulf of Orosei and of Last Interglacial (~120,000 to 130,000 years) age. Areas where this shoreline occurs a few meters above present sea level are assumed to have been tectonically relatively stable. D. A more recent erosion notch from the same area as (C) probably formed during the slow and gradual local sea level rise of the past 7000 years.

E   F

G   H

E. Submerged speleothems from a cave on the island of Argentarola, Tuscany. The speleothems developed when the cave was above sea level but growth was interrupt and overgrown with marine encrustations during a subsequent flooding phase. F. An erosion notch from western Crete (near Balos) of Late Holocene age. The notch is above present formation level and is indicative of a rapid uplift event. G. The incomplete Roman fishtank at Phalasarna (Crete), now at ~ 6 m above sea level, and probably abandoned because of land uplift following the 365 AD earthquake (Note the fault that cuts across it). H. The partly excavated and now uplifted Roman harbor of Phalasarna, circa 50 BC, showing the quay and in situ bollards. Marine crustaceans (on the shaded wall) suggest that the uplift occurred after about 1600 years ago, at the time of a major earthquake at 365 AD and associated tsunami. The archaeological and geological evidence illustrated in F, G, and H point to long-term episodic uplift of western Crete at rates of several mm/year.

I. Erosion notches in limestone cliffs of the Perachora Peninsula (Gulf of Corinth) indicating a series of episodic uplift events during the past few thousand years. J. Submerged temple foundations from Hellenic to early Christian Periods at Kenchria on the Saronic Gulf, less than 20 km east off Perachora. Here the evidence points to rising sea level during the past 3000 years. Trends of local change can change rapidly from locality to locality. K. Aerial view of Torre Astura (near Rome) showing the submerged remains of extensive fishtanks (image from www.bing.com/maps). Fishtanks are found in many locations around the Mediterranean and most abundantly on the Thyrhennian coast of Italy near Rome and date mainly from the Augustan Epoch. Their construction methods, and functions are well documented in classical writings of Pliny, Columella, and others. Their functionality is tightly controlled by the tides at the time of construction and the location of inflow-outflow channels and other tidally-controlled features, above or below present sea level, provide an excellent indicator of sea level since the time of construction. L. Oblique view of the same location as in K.

M. The outer walls of a fishtank at La Banca (near Torre Astura). The tops of the foundations of the walls were constructed above sea level to protect the inner structures from wave-action. Remains of timber posts inserted into the foundations permit the structures to be radiocarbon dated and confirms the Augustan date. Here sea level today lies above the functional levels of the channels and sluice gates controlling flow into the tanks, indicating that locally sea level has risen by ~ 1.5 m since the time of construction. N. A partly cleaned in situ sluice gate in one of the channels controlling flow into and out off the tank at La Banca. The vertical side of the cleaned stone (or lead in some other fishtanks) contains holes to allow exchange of water between the sea and tank (the grey area at the level of the black and lower markers on the 20 cm division measuring rod). Sliding grooves in the walls (see particularly the one on the left-hand side) allows the gate to be raised. The lower level of the channel is marked by the black stone (of volcanic origin, possibly from the nearly Alban Hills, that is more resistant to biological erosion) beneath the gate. The top of the wall on the right hand side marks the lowest level *crepido*. O. A fixed sluice gate in position without sliding groves from Ventotene Island. P. Two levels of *crepido*, with the lowest level partly buried by sediment and the outer wall of a fishtank.

Q

R

Q. The Roman Epoch fishtank from near Caesarea, Israel, with the channels still at sea level. In the distance, where the man is standing, there is a coralline algal rim that marks the position of present sea level and which contains information on changes typically for the last few hundred years. R. The remains of the Roman market, often referred to as the temple of Serapis, Pozzuoli, with marine borers in the column at ~ 7-8 m above present sea level that indicate that the area has undergone successive subsidence and uplift since the time of construction associated with the volcanism within the Flegrei Caldera. Photos by Marco Anzidei (INGV), Fabrizio Antonioli (ENEA) and the author unless otherwise noted.

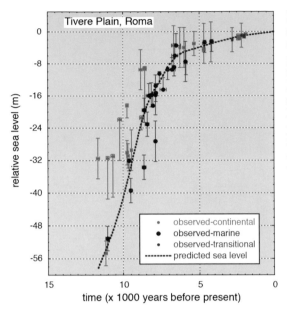

Fig. 14. Comparison of predicted (red dashed line) and observed sea levels for the Tivere Plain near Rome during the past 12,000 years. The blue points are marine observations and sea level must lie above these points. The green points are terrestrial markers and sea level must lie below these levels. The two brown points are from the transition from terrestrial to marine conditions, formed during the earliest stages of the marine transgression.

the tides at their time of construction. Today most of these fish tanks along the Tyrrhenian coast are submerged (Fig. 13) and from the recovered sluice gates, channels and foot walks (*crepidines*) we have been able to establish that sea level has risen locally by ~ 1.3 m over the past 2000 years. Much of this rise is part of the background isostatic signal but, by comparing this with 100-year tide gauge records from nearby sites we have been able to ascertain that the present rate of sea level rise, of about 1.5 mm/year recorded at nearby tide gauges, is a relatively recent phenomenon that cannot be attributed to past geological processes.

This is as far as I can go today. What I have tried to do is provide some insight into the processes that have caused sea level to change through time and how the study of these processes may lead to a better understanding of problems that are of interest to different areas of science and in some cases important to society. I have also indicated several times that it is still a work in progress. I am coming to the end of my career and I am hoping that the Balzan funding is going to be able to help a new group of researchers continue with this work. If that is successful then I think the Balzan Prize money will have been very worthwhile. Thank you very much for this opportunity.

REFERENCES AND NOTES

1. GAPOSCHKIN, E.M. and LAMBECK, K., 1971, *Earth's gravity field to sixteenth degree and station coordinates from satellite and terrestrial data*, «J. Geophys. Res.», 76, 4855-4883.

2. LAMBECK, K., CAZENAVE, A. and BALMINO, G., 1974, *Solid Earth and ocean tides estimated from satellite orbit analyses*, «Rev. Geoph. Space Phys.», 12, 421-434.

3. LAMBECK, K., 1980, *The Earth's Variable Rotation: Geophysical Causes and Consequences*, Cambridge University Press, 450 pp.

4. STEPHENSON, R. and LAMBECK, K., 1985, *Isostatic response of the lithosphere with in-plane stress: application to central Australia*, «J. Geophys. Res.», 90, 8581-8588.

5. NAKADA, M. and LAMBECK, K., 1987, *Glacial rebound and relative sea level variations: a new appraisal. Geophys*, «J. Roy. astr. Soc.», 90, 171-224.

6. SIVAN, D., WDOWINSKI, S., LAMBECK, K., GALILI, E. and RABAN, A., 2001, *Holocene sea level changes along the Mediterranean coast of Israel, based on archaeological observations and numerical model*, «Palaeogeogr. Palaeoclimatol. Palaeoecol», 167, 101-117.

7. CAPUTO, M., PIERI, L., 1972, in G. SCHMIEDT, *Il livello antico del mar Tirreno. Testimonianze da resti archeologici*, Olschki, Firenze, 323 pp.
    LAMBECK, K., ANTONIOLI, F., PURCELL, A., SILENZI, S., 2004a, *Sea level change along the Italian coast for the past 10,000 yr*, «Quaternary Science Reviews», 23, 1567-1598.

8. LAMBECK, K., PURCELL, A., FUNDER, S., KJÆR, K., LARSEN, E., MÖLLER, P., 2006, *Constraints on the Late Saalian to early Middle Weichselian ice sheet of Eurasia from field data and rebound modelling*, «Borcas», 35(3), 539-575.
    LAMBECK, K., PURCELL, A., ZHAO, J. and SVENSSON, N-O., 2010a, *The Scandinavian Ice Sheet: from MIS 4 to the end of the Last Glacial Maximum*, «Boreas», 39(2), 410-435.
    DUTTON, A., LAMBECK, K., 2012, *Ice volume and sea level during the Last Interglacial*, «Science», 337, 216-219.

9. LAMBECK, K., 1996, *Shoreline reconstructions for the Persian Gulf since the last glacial Maximum*, «Earth Planet. Sci. Lett.», 142, 43-57.

10. LAMBECK, K., PURCELL, A., FLEMMING, N.C., VITA-FINZI, C., ALSHAREKH, A.M., BAILEY, G.N., 2011, *Sea level and shoreline reconstructions for the Red Sea: isostatic and tectonic considerations and implications for hominin migration out of Africa*, «Quaternary Science Reviews», 30, 3542-3574.

11. LAMBECK, K., and CHAPPELL, J., 2001, *Sea Level Change through the last Glacial Cycle*, «Science», 292, 679-686.

12. ZWARTZ, D., BIRD, M., STONE, J. and LAMBECK, K., 1998, *Holocene sea level change and ice sheet history in the Vestfold Hills, East Antarctica*, «Earth Planet. Sci. Lett.», 155, 131-145.

13. Agenzia nazionale per le nuove tecnologie, l'energia e lo sviluppo economico sostenibile, Rome.

14. Istituto Nazionale di Geofisica e Vulcanologia, Rome.
15. LAMBECK, K., ANTONIOLI, F., ANZIDEI, M., FERRANTI, L., LEONI, G., SCICCHITANO, G., SILENZI, S., 2010b, *Sea level change along the Italian coast during the Holocene and projections for the future*, «Quaternary International», 232, 250-257.
16. LAMBECK, K., ANTONIOLI, F., PURCELL, A., SILENZI, S., 2004b, *Sea level change along the Italian coast for the past 10,000 yr*, «Quaternary Science Reviews», 23, 1567-1598.
17. LAMBECK, K., ANTONIOLI, F., ANZIDEI, M., 2010c, *Sea level change along the Tyrrhenian coast from early Holocene to the present*, in *Il Bacino del Tevere*. Atti dei Convegni Lincei 254, Accademia Nazionale dei Lincei, Rome, pp. 11-26.
18. HSÜ, K.J., CITA, M.B., RYAN, W.B.F., 1973, *The origin of the Mediterranean evaporites*, Init. Repts. DSDP, vol. 13. U.S. Govt. Printing Office, Washington, D.C., pp. 1203-1231.
19. «Il Messaggero», Rome, 17 September 2013.

DISCUSSION AND QUESTIONS

Giuseppe Orombelli: My task here is to promote debate but first of all I would like to thank Professor Lambeck for such a clearly presented lecture on a topic which is both highly interesting and also highly intriguing and complicated because it connects several parts of the Earth's system. I work on the relationship between changes in sea level and climate in addition to sea level changes and ice sheets. Professor Lambeck in his lecture showed several examples of the information that we can obtain on past climate and environmental changes by studying changes in sea level. He illustrated for instance the development of the Scandinavian and the Laurentide ice sheets during the Last Glacial Maximum. He also spoke about the connection between changes in sea level and archaeology or – if you wish – human evolution and the history of man. This is important because sea level changes greatly affected the land bridges that previously connected continents together. So this topic is useful both for interpreting the past and also for understanding the present. Thus I would like to solicit questions regarding the present including the rate of sea level rise, which is obviously very relevant for the future! Before doing that however I would like to get in an introductory question or two. Professor Lambeck what are the major contributions that sea level studies have brought to the understanding of climate and environmental changes in the past?

Kurt Lambeck: I think the first thing such studies are providing is a quantification of the relationship between climate and the ice sheets through the sea level part. For example, we have not known how thick ice sheets were in the past. There have been glaciologically-based estimates but now we have good constraints on that from the sea level analyses. I believe we have got that problem partly solved. I have presented a model for the ice-earth-ocean interactions that works well for the last 20,000 years. Now, from the principles I have learned from this I can extrapolate back in time. We have done that for Scandinavia and for northern Russia, for example, and one of the results is confirmation of the concept that at the onset of a new glacial cycle the activity seems to be all in the East: with the ice forming in the Kara Sea area moving onto the land, moving south, and back and forth until it reaches its maximum at the so called Saalian, covering large parts of northern Europe as far east as the Russian Taymyr. If this is correct it tells us that the Arctic Ocean plays a very important role because that movement back and forth is only possible if the Arctic Ocean is open so as to provide a good supply of moisture. I try not to speculate in cases like this but one can ask the question: What happens if the Arctic Ocean opens up fully today? Is this going to produce a flow of cold air in contact with comparatively warm water into that northern part? Is it going to change precipitation? In the absence of other forcing, would it actually result in the regrowth of ice up there?

Giuseppe Orombelli: I know that you worked also on the last interglacial, what about the ice sheets during the last interglacial? Can you hypothesise what might have been responsible for a 4 to 5 meters plus rise in the sea level?

Kurt Lambeck: I thought a year or so ago that we had that problem solved, mainly from the western Australia record where there is over 15 hundred kilometers of fossil coral reef that identify sea levels at about the same level of ~ 3-4 m and where, behind the reefs you can see old lagoon structure with morphological evidence of where the sea level was. This is what led to the 4 to 5 meters that we favoured recently in *Science*. I had heard about some corals in the Seychelles that Barbara Wohlfarth from Stockholm had dated some years back and which were reported to be 8 or 9 meters above sea level. So I made the mistake of suggesting to one of my colleagues to go there and observe and date them. And they are indeed at those elevations and of last interglacial age. What does this difference mean? 4 to 5 meters we can accommodate by a large part of melting of Greenland – we know from the ice core data that about half of the ice sheet has gone – and we can probably accept a few meters of melt water from West Antarctica (although this remains an open question) so that one can explain the 4 to 5 meters as being the response of those ice sheets to a global warming of a few degrees Celsius. But 8 meters or 9 meters, as the Seychelles data requires, changes that picture totally because then we had to have a large melt component from East Antarctica as well and for which there is no substantial observational or model evidence. I am reluctant to overthrow my good western Australian record with one observation from the Seychelles and I am tempted to say that perhaps there are some strange tectonics going on there. We need to corroborate that evidence from other sites. As I said before, I thought I had the problem solved but I am back to square one.

Giuseppe Orombelli: Thank you. Now I would like to open the floor to questions from the public concerning this part of the topic before handing over to my colleague for the part concerned with geophysics.

Maria Bianca Cita Sironi: According to your in depth experience what do you think is more reliable, the deep sea record where you have no tectonics or the record from the coastal areas? On land you may have passive continental margin where sea level changes are usually well expressed. One problem is if you have to go to active continental margins that are strongly affected by neo tectonics, how do you discriminate tectonic signals from the glacio-eustatic signals?

Kurt Lambeck: That is an important question. For those of you who are not familiar with it, I have been talking about direct observations of sea level change as recorded locally in coastal environments. There is another way of looking at global changes in sea level, looking at the oxygen isotopic composition of sediments on the deep sea floor. This isotopic composition reflects the ratio of fresh water, added into the ocean from melting ice sheets, and salt water, with the freshwater, originating as snow precipitation, having a higher content of the light oxygen isotope than the ocean. If you can measure fluctuations in this isotopic ratio then you have a first order estimate of the sea level change globally. The trouble is that there are other factors that contribute to this ratio, temperature for example or if you are looking at it in near-closed basins like the Mediterranean or Red Sea you may have local hydraulic conditions as well. Hence one of our aims is to try and develop a sea level record that is totally independent of the isotope information and then to compare it with the isotopic record to calibrate the latter and to use it to interpolate and extrapolate from the sea level observations. To use the example of the Red Sea cores, people have speculated that there are oscillations in sea level during the last interglacial of the order of 5 meters or more on timescales of hundreds of years. Now physically I find that implausible because imagine the situation today. How can you produce a 5 meter sea level rise? The ice sheets would have had to have melted rapidly in Greenland and in West Antarctica on sub-millennium time scales. Perhaps that is possible but then they have to be rebuilt again within the same short period. I have a suspicion that that tells us more about the noise, the precision of the isotopic sea level interferences than it does about the real changes. This is where independent high-resolution observations of sea level change during this interval become most important. Having said that, the isotopic record is extremely important for looking at the longer period cycles and that has been a marvellous piece of work with which I have no quibbles whatsoever.

Giuseppe Orombelli: One might be interested in knowing something about the present rate of sea level rise and the accuracy of future rates. We know that the IPCC (Intergovernmental Panel on Climate Change) report will be published shortly. Professor Lambeck may have something to tell us?

Kurt Lambeck: The conclusions from the instrumental records have not changed very much from the previous report, showing that there has been a substantial sea level rise in the last hundred years, which from comparisons with our earlier fish-tank analysis for example and also with some very recent evidence from salt-marsh deposits, indicates that this rise could only have started about a hundred years ago. The recognition has set in nevertheless that superimposed upon the secular rise of the last 100 or so years, there are decadal-scale cycles of change so that linear extrapolation is a very dangerous thing to do, as is any other mathematical extrapolation that does not contain the physics of sea level change. For the last two decades we have records of sea level change from satellite altimetry and this has been a remarkable achievement. That record suggests that there has been an upturn in the rate of rise starting about 20 years ago and as we see it also in the tide gauge record something happened there. But if you look at the whole record critically you find similar periods where sea level has gone up faster than the 100 year average and then slowed down again. So I do not think one should extrapolate that 3 mm per year but one can probably safely extrapolate 1.5 to 2 mm per year.

Giuseppe Orombelli: I will now hand over to Professor Carlo Doglioni who is much more expert in geophysics and geodynamics.

Carlo Doglioni: Professor Lambeck, thank you for your very informative lecture. Let us move down deeper in the earth now and my first question concerns your viscosity results that we were discussing before. Viscosity is the resistance to shearing, it measures how a fluid reacts to a shear but with the glacial isostatic adjustment we measure only vertical movements which just load and unload the mantle without having an indication of what is the shear for example in the low velocity zone. That is very important because the values which are obtained from glacial isostatic rebound are used to calculate the viscosity of the upper mantle and as you know, as we were discussing, if there is a thin layer – let's say – 50 kilometers thick it is practically invisible to the loading of a 3,000 kilometer wide ice cap. I think the contribution of such studies is fundamental but I am afraid that the viscosity values which are obtained do not give us enough information about the viscosity under shear in the top part of the upper mantle, could you comment on that?

Kurt Lambeck: As usual you have hit the nail right on the head because that is a very important question and I did not want to dwell too much on the viscosity results because of the complexity of their interpretation. What we are usually very careful to say is that our estimates are effective viscosities. They are parameters that describe a particular class of observations and you have to be careful about how you apply them to a totally different class of problem, in your case, mantle convection. You are saying correctly that our numbers may not be relevant if you want to examine the extent to which the lithosphere can be decoupled from the upper mantle for example. We have to take our limited approach because there is no geological observation of horizontal displacements in response to glacial rebound. There is a geodetic observation from the modern-day very high precision positioning with GPS, where for example, we begin to see around Scandinavia a pattern of outward radiating horizontal displacements. But the current GPS observations and analysis methods are not yet adequate to be able to invert the data for the horizontal shear viscosity. There are also issues of contribution to this pattern from the North American ice sheet and the extent to which stresses are transmitted across the mid-Atlantic ridge, contributions to the displacements from other tectonic processes and definition of long-term stable reference frames. It is going to take some time but I am sure that we will get there.

Carlo Doglioni: Well, I think this is a crucial issue because most of the geodynamic evidence indicates that there is a decoupling between the lithosphere and the underlying mantle but if you apply a viscosity of 10^{20} Pascal-second the viscosity would be so high that the decoupling would be inhibited. We do see decoupling so from shear way splitting, the Hawaii plume, many other indications about that and there are more and more indications that the low velocity zone is a very low velocity in terms of shear waves and this would suggest a much lower viscosity than so far expected from glacial isostatic rebound.

Kurt Lambeck: Actually this is a very useful discussion and raises some issues that we will need to follow up on. I am trying to recall the results from analysis of the displacement fields following the large recent earthquakes. These lead to viscosities that are distinctly lower than what we get from the glacial rebound and we have been interpreting these in terms of transient creep behaviour but I now wonder, listening to your question, whether it is actually because one is a vertical response and the other is an horizontal one. So you may have touched upon something that is very useful.

Carlo Doglioni: Yes, you were talking about nonlinear rheology. I mean we may have also a strength weakening and it depends from the wavelength of the force which is acting on the lithosphere so this may be important and the wavelength of the oscillations that you are describing in terms of glaciation is – let us say – a very short wavelength with respect to the tectonic. There is another topical issue for example that the upper mantle particularly the top of the asthenosphere is considered a superadiabatic condition so the temperature could be much higher than so far expected. In fact evidence suggests that the amount of melting may be even higher than 2% or 3% so this would even lower the viscosity in the upper mantle but the question is still that the isostatic rebound from deglaciation is not able to see a thin layer. That was the channel flow by Cathles in 1975.

Kurt Lambeck: If it is a very thin layer, as you said in your earlier question, the stress is just propagated straight across it and you don't see the effects of it. We have done some experiments with one of the well constrained ice sheets, the British ice sheet. It is a small ice sheet so it does not stress the lower mantle and you have then got a direct upper mantle signal. From that we have suggested that there is some viscosity layering in the upper mantle but that the increase with depth is no more than a factor of 2 or 3, going from perhaps 2 or 3 times 10^{20} to 5 or 6 times 10^{20}, it is not terribly dramatic. The problem we have is that there is a limit to how far we can push the rebound models and I think I have gone about as far as I am prepared to go. This is because there is a fundamental problem regarding inadequate knowledge on the ice sheets. Many people have been doing lots of fancy modelling, showing all sorts of stratification in the mantle using the nearest ice sheet at hand, ignoring the fact that these ice models are quite uncertain.

Carlo Doglioni: Are there any more questions please?

Question from the audience: A question about sea level markers. We used for the last interglacial the higher sea level marker. Do you think it is possible to use also the lower sea level marker, I mean the position at which the sea level was at in the Last Glacial Maximum, as a way to reconstruct the behaviour of the crust and so of the isostatic and tectonic movements? Because on the continental margin we are able to depict what is the maximum depth at which the sea level was or at which the sea level was eroding the seafloor, so can – in your opinion – that bring a new field for establishing the behaviour of different parts of the crust and so to prove the models for the vertical movement of the crust?

Kurt Lambeck: Certainly, the variation that we see for say the last interglacial sea levels around the world are also true for the sea levels at Glacial Maxima so if you could map the sea levels at the time of the Glacial Maximum around the Mediterranean for example here you would see variations of the order of 30 meters from 100 to 130 meters. If you could map that, that would be a very powerful observation, not only for the Earth rheology determination but also for estimating changes in global ice volume. You see the isostatic effects to some degree in the Gulf of Lion, for example, where the Last Glacial Maximum is at a much shallower depth than the usual 125, 130 meters that you see at many continental margins. If you can recall one of the figures I showed, you saw there has been a bunching up of the contours of equal sea level change in that area. The problem with the Glacial Maximum data is that you may be able to identify an old shoreline but the age is often quite uncertain. If you can come up with a good data set I am sure I can find an explanation.

Carlo Doglioni: Thank you Professor Lambeck, any other questions? No questions so I will hand over to Professor Maria Bianca Cita Sironi.

Maria Bianca Cita Sironi: I have a last question: is your work applied research or pure research?

Kurt Lambeck: I will give a very glib answer, though in my mind it is a true one: I do not see a difference between pure and applied research, there is only good research and bad research!

Alberto Quadrio Curzio: I have to say that I will also lay claim to the last question posed by Professor Maria Bianca Cita Sironi, since I mentioned to her that, being an economist, it seems to me there is quite a lot of difference between applied and theoretical research: with applied research you do money, with theoretical research you do not do money. So many thanks indeed for this splendid lecture and I am sure that this will make a wonderful fifth volume in the series of Annual Balzan Lectures.

Kurt Lambeck: Thank you for the opportunity to have been able to address you in this distinguished institution, the Accademia Nazionale dei Lincei.

Accademia Nazionale dei Lincei: Kurt Lambeck's presentation.

From left to right: Kurt Lambeck, Maria Bianca Cita Sironi,
Lamberto Maffei and Alberto Quadrio Curzio.

Accademia Nazionale dei Lincei: the Audience, Discussion and Questions.

KURT LAMBECK

BIOGRAPHICAL AND BIBLIOGRAPHICAL DATA

KURT LAMBECK, born in Utrecht, the Netherlands, on 20 September 1941, is since 1956 an Australian citizen.

Emeritus Professor at the Australian National University since 2008; Blaise Pascal Professor at the École Normale Supérieure, Paris (2011-2012); former President of the Federation of Asian Science Academies and Associations (2009-2013); former President of the Australian Academy of Science (2006-2010).

He obtained a B.Surv. (Hons. 1, University Medal) from the Faculty of Engineering, University of New South Wales, Australia, in 1963, a D.Phil. from the University of Oxford in 1967 and a D.Sc. from the University of Oxford in 1976. He worked as a Geodesist at the Smithsonian Astrophysical Observatory and at Harvard University, Cambridge, Massachusetts, USA, from 1967 to 1970. From 1970 to 1973 he was Directeur scientifique du Groupe de Recherche de Géodésie spatiale, Observatoire de Paris, and from 1973 to 1977 Professeur Associé, Département des Sciences de la Terre, University of Paris VII, and Institut de Physique du Globe de Paris. From 1977 to 2007 he was Professor of Geophysics at the Research School of Earth Sciences at the Australian National University, including ten years as Director of the Research School of Earth Sciences. He has held visiting appointments in Belgium, Britain, Canada, France, Greece, the Netherlands, Norway and Sweden.

He has been a member of the Australian Academy of Science since 1984, Fellow of the Royal Society of London since 1994 and of the Royal Society of New South Wales, Australia, since 2010, and a Foreign Member of the Royal Netherlands Academy of Arts and Sciences since 1993, of the Norwegian Academy of Science and Letters since 1994, of the Academia Europæa since 1999, of the Académie des

Sciences, Institut de France, since 2005, of the US National Academy of Sciences since 2009, and of the American Academy of Arts and Sciences since 2010.

He has published more than 300 papers on subjects in geophysics, geology, geodesy, space science, celestial mechanics, environmental geoscience and glaciology, as well as the following two books:

– *The Earth's Variable Rotation: Geophysical Causes and Consequences*. Cambridge University Press, 1980, Cambridge University Press Virtual Publishing, 2005.
– *Geophysical Geodesy: The Slow Deformations of the Earth*. Oxford University Press, Oxford, 1988.

SEA LEVEL CHANGE DURING GLACIAL CYCLES

Adviser for the Balzan General Prize Committee: Enric Banda

Sea levels have changed throughout the Earth's history, and have impacted on the movements of species between land masses, including human movements over the more recent period of the past 100,000 or so years. The causes include tectonic and climate processes, and over the past million years it is the latter, with the cyclic growth and decay of the great ice sheets, that has been most important. Understanding how sea level has changed helps understand the fundamental processes that have shaped the earth through time. It is a truly interdisciplinary area of research involving the disciplines of solid-earth geophysics, geology and geochemistry, underpinned by physics and mathematics, with implications for past climates and human pre-history. The research component of the Balzan Prize addresses some important elements of this broad subject.

RESEARCH THEMES

1. *Geophysical modelling of interactions between ice sheets, the solid earth and sea level.* When ice sheets melt or grow, they stress the earth and change the gravity field, which together leads to a complex spatial pattern of sea level change. Modelling of these interactions rests on a number of hypotheses that need testing, something that is now possible because of both enhanced computational facilities and observational data. Numerical modelling developments include refinement of our models through improved characterisation of the Earth's rheological parameters and improved inversions of field data for inferring the ice sheet history. One of the goals is to develop a version of

the numerical models suitable for use by 'non-experts' so as to make the methodology available to geologists and archaeologists. Another goal is to develop the next iteration of ice sheet models with a particular focus on the Antarctic ice sheet, which up to now has played a rather passive role in the discussion of past sea levels, despite it being important in assessing the future of this ice sheet in a framework of a warming planet. Other targets include an improved ice sheet model for southern Greenland and improvements in the North American ice sheet model. These models provide improved reference points for testing climate models under conditions very different from today as well as the basis for palaeogeographic reconstructions during recent glacial cycles to explore possible constraints on human migrations.

2. *Past interglacials as analogs of the present interglacial.* The past interglacials that occur about every 110,000 years are periods when climate was similar to today and sea levels were close to present-day values. The last interglacial is particularly important because its traces are best preserved in the geological record. Its climate was similar to today, but possibly a few degrees warmer, and sea levels were 4-6 meters higher than today. But the precise timing of this occurrence and any variability within the interglacial interval remains poorly constrained. Yet this information is important in the context of current climate change debate for understanding the sensitivity of ice sheets to changes in temperature. Field sites from which we have preliminary information include: western and northern Australia, the Seychelles and the Mediterranean. Earlier interglacials will also be examined including the Pliocene (~ 3 million years ago), when the global glacial-interglacial cycles were markedly different from those of the past 800,000 years.

3. *The present interglacial (the Holocene).* Ocean volumes have remained approximately constant during the past 6000 years, but periodically the argument arises that large amplitude (1-2 m) changes have occurred within relatively short time periods (a few hundred years). If correct, this has major implications for the instability of the climate system when the planet is not in an ice age. There are many reasons why this question remains debated. One is of the nature of the observational evidence. Another is land movement caused by tec-

tonic and global dynamic processes. A third is the ongoing interaction between the past ice sheets and the solid earth and oceans. We address these issues to arrive at what should be a definitive answer to the question of sea level (and hence climate) stability or instability during interglacial periods.

THE RESEARCH PLAN

The funding has enabled a research associate to be appointed for 2 years at the Australian National University (ANU) to work on the modelling aspects of the various components of the earth-ocean-ice system. The appointee, Dr Anthony Purcell, has experience in this research area, so as to build on past work. A second appointment of a Post Doctoral Fellow, Dr Hélène Rouby, has been made together with the École Normale Supérieure (ENS) in Paris to work on the analysis of sea level data to develop high-resolution models for sea level change in low- and mid-latitude regions. This is part of a longer-term proposal to transfer the ANU software and experience to ENS for use by French researchers and to introduce a more complex mantle rheology into our models.

Support has also been provided to Ms Ye-Ying Sun from the University of Hong Kong (UHK) to work as a Balzan Student at the Australian National University (ANU) during 2013 compiling and analyzing sea level data from South East Asia, from Malaysia to Japan, and learning the elements of geophysical modelling. This work is significant for both the global studies and for examining the past subsidence rates of the large east and southeast Asian river deltas. Contributions to two field projects have been made to permit students to extend their PhD work. One is a project with Ms Brigid Morrison from the University of Tasmania to collect further core samples from sites in Tasmania, and to provide radiocarbon dating, to examine the rise of sea level during the past 7000 years. The significance of this study is that it may answer questions about the role of Antarctica to the global sea level change since the last glacial maximum. The other project has provided support for PhD student Belinda Dechnik from Sydney University to participate in fieldwork in the Seychelles that examines earlier interglacial reefs that are now above sea level. These projects focus on specific scientific targets that bring together young and experienced researchers in selected field environments, in the requisite laboratory methods and in computational methods. Further field projects involving young researchers in Australia are being examined and will be gradually introduced over the next two years.

Sea level is an important component of the four-yearly Intergovernmental Panel on Climate Change assessment of the science of climate change. The Final Draft of the Working Group 1 report was delivered in May 2013. It highlights many of the important questions for which better answers are required. It is expected that by the Balzan Foundation research inspired the project will contribute significantly to providing useful answers.

RESEARCHERS

Belinda Dechnik
Brigid Morrison
Anthony Purcell
Hélène Rouby
Ye-Ying Sun

PROFILES

THE INTERNATIONAL BALZAN FOUNDATION

The *International Balzan Foundation "Prize"* aims to promote, throughout the world, culture, science, and the most meritorious initiatives in the cause of humanity, peace and fraternity among peoples, regardless of nationality, race or creed. This aim is attained through the annual award of prizes in two general academic categories: literature, the moral sciences and the arts; medicine and the physical, mathematical and natural sciences. Specific subjects for the awarding of Prizes are chosen on an annual basis.

Nominations for these prizes are received at the Foundation's request from the world's leading academic institutions. Candidates are selected by the *General Prize Committee*, composed of eminent European scholars and scientists. Prizewinners must allocate half of the Prize to research work, preferably involving young researchers.

At intervals of not less than three years, the Balzan Foundation also awards a prize of varying amounts for Humanity, Peace and Fraternity among Peoples.

The *International Balzan Foundation "Prize"* attains its financial means from the *International Balzan Foundation "Fund"* which administers Eugenio Balzan's estate.

THE ACCADEMIA NAZIONALE DEI LINCEI

The *Accademia Nazionale dei Lincei*, founded in 1603 by the Roman-Umbrian aristocrat Federico Cesi and three other young scholars, Anastasio De Filiis, Johannes Eck and Francesco Stelluti, is the oldest scientific academy in the world. It promotes academic excellence through its Fellows whose earliest members included, among many other renowned names, Galileo Galilei.

The Academy's mission is "to promote, coordinate, integrate and disseminate scientific knowledge in its highest expressions in the context of cultural unity and universality".

The activities of the Academy are carried out according to two guiding principles that complement one another: to enrich academic knowledge and disseminate the fruits of this. To this end, the Accademia Nazionale dei Lincei organises national and international conferences, meetings and seminars and encourages academic cooperation and exchange between scientists and scholars at the national and international level. The Academy promotes research activities and missions, confers awards and grants, publishes the reports of its own sessions and the notes and records presented therein, as well as the proceedings of its own conferences, meetings and seminars.

The Academy further provides – either upon request or on its own initiative – advice to public institutions and when appropriate drafts relevant reports. Since 1992, the Academy has served as an official adviser to the President of the Italian Republic in relation to scholarly and scientific matters.

THE SWISS ACADEMIES OF ARTS AND SCIENCES

The Association of the *Swiss Academies of Arts and Sciences* includes the Swiss Academy of Sciences (SCNAT), the Swiss Academy of Humanities and Social Sciences (SAHS), the Swiss Academy of Medical Sciences (SAMS), and the Swiss Academy of Engineering Sciences (SATW) as well as the two Centres for Excellence TA-SWISS and Science et Cité. Their collaboration is focused on methods of anticipating future trends, ethics and the dialogue between science, the arts and society. It is the aim of the *Swiss Academies of Arts and Sciences* to develop an equal dialogue between academia and society and to advise Government on scientifically based, socially relevant questions. The academies stand for an open and pluralistic understanding of science and the arts. Over the long-term, they mutually commit to resolving interdisciplinary questions in the following fields:
-   They offer knowledge and expertise in relation to socially relevant subjects in the fields of Education, Research and Technology.
-   They adhere to the concept of ethically-based responsibility in gaining and applying scientific and humanistic knowledge.
-   They build bridges between Academia, Government and Society.

AGREEMENTS ON COLLABORATION BETWEEN THE INTERNATIONAL BALZAN FOUNDATION "PRIZE", THE SWISS ACADEMIES OF ARTS AND SCIENCES AND THE ACCADEMIA NAZIONALE DEI LINCEI

(Hereafter referred to as the 'Balzan', the 'Swiss Academies' and the 'Lincei', respectively)

The main points of the agreements between the Balzan, the Swiss Academies and the Lincei are the following:

1) The promotion of the Balzan Prize and the presentation of the Prizewinners through the academies' channels of communication, in Italy and Switzerland as well as abroad. By virtue of the relations of the Swiss Academies and the Lincei with academies of other countries and with international academic organizations, they will contribute to more widespread circulation of news related to the Balzan;

2) On the occasion of the Awards ceremony of the Balzan Prize, held on alternating years in Berne and Rome, each academy will contribute to the academic organization of an interdisciplinary Forum, in the course of which the Prizewinners of that year will present their academic work and discuss it with other academics proposed by the academies. Furthermore, in the years when the ceremony is held in Rome, one of the Prizewinners will give the Balzan Annual Lecture in Switzerland, and when the ceremony is held in Berne, the Balzan Annual Lecture will be organized at the headquarters of the Lincei in Rome;

3) The academies will contribute to a series of publications in English (ideally with summaries in Italian, German and French), created by the Balzan, with the collaboration of the Balzan Prizewinners.

To promote and supervise all these initiatives, two Commissions have been set up, one between the Balzan and the Swiss Academies (composed of its President originally Professor René Dändliker followed by Professor Peter Suter, then Heinz Gutscher and now Thierry Courvoisier, Dr. Markus Zürcher and Professor Meier-Abt) and another between the Balzan and the Lincei (composed of Professors Sergio Carrà, Lellia Cracco Ruggini and formerly Claudio Leonardi†, now Carlo Ossola). Both commissions are chaired by Professor Alberto Quadrio Curzio as a representative of the Balzan, which is also represented by Professors Enrico Decleva and Paolo Matthiae, while the Balzan Secretary General, Dr. Suzanne Werder, has been appointed Secretary of both Commissions.

Embassy of Italy in Washington; Appointed by an inter-ministerial decree of the Italian Ministry of Foreign Affairs and Ministry of Education, Universities and Research as the representative of the Italian Republic on the Balzan Foundation "Prize" Board

PAOLO MATTHIAE   *Member*
Professor Emeritus of Archaeology and History of Art of the Ancient Near East at the University of Rome "La Sapienza"; Fellow of the Accademia Nazionale dei Lincei, Rome; Appointed by the Balzan General Prize Committee as their representative on the Balzan Foundation "Prize" Board

ALBERTO QUADRIO CURZIO   *Member*
Professor Emeritus of Political Economy as well as Founder and President of the scientific Council of the Research Centre on Economic Analysis (CRANEC) at the Università Cattolica del Sacro Cuore, Milan; Vice-President and President of the Class of Moral, Historical and Philological Sciences of the Accademia Nazionale dei Lincei, Rome

GENERAL PRIZE COMMITTEE

(December 2013)

SALVATORE VECA	*Chairman* Professor of Political Philosophy and Vice-Rector of the Institute for Advanced Study (IUSS), Pavia
ENRIC BANDA	*Vice-Chairman* Research Professor of Geophysics at the Institute of Earth Sciences in Barcelona, Spanish Council for Scientific Research (CSIC); former Secretary General of the European Science Foundation, Strasbourg; former President of Euroscience, Strasbourg
PAOLO MATTHIAE	*Vice-Chairman* Professor Emeritus of Archaeology and History of Art of the Ancient Near East at the University of Rome "La Sapienza"; Fellow of the Accademia Nazionale dei Lincei, Rome
ETIENNE GHYS	*Member* Research Director at the Centre National de la Recherche Scientifique, Pure and Applied Mathematics Unit, École Normale Supérieure de Lyon; Member of the Académie des sciences, Institut de France, Paris
H. CHARLES J. GODFRAY	*Member* Hope Professor of Zoology at the University of Oxford and Fellow of Jesus College; Fellow of the Royal Society
BENGT GUSTAFSSON	*Member* Professor Emeritus of Theoretical Astrophysics at the University of Uppsala; Member of the Royal Swedish Academy of Science, the Royal Danish Academy of

Sciences and Letters, and the Norwegian Academy of Sciences and Letters

JULES A. HOFFMANN

Member
Distinguished Class Research Director at the Centre National de la Recherche Scientifique (Emeritus), Institute of Molecular and Cellular Biology, Strasbourg; Professor at the University of Strasbourg; former President of the Académie des sciences, Institut de France, Paris; 2011 Nobel Prize for Physiology or Medicine

LUCIANO MAIANI

Member
Professor Emeritus of Theoretical Physics at the University of Rome "La Sapienza"; Fellow of the Accademia Nazionale dei Lincei, Rome, and of the American Physical Society

THOMAS MAISSEN

Member
Director of the German Historical Institute in Paris; Chair in Early Modern History at the University of Heidelberg; Member of the Heidelberger Akademie der Wissenschaften

ERWIN NEHER

Member
Professor Emeritus, Max Planck Institute for Biophysical Chemistry, Göttingen; Member of the Academia Europaea; Foreign Associate of the US National Academy of Sciences and of the Royal Society, London; 1991 Nobel Prize for Physiology or Medicine

ANTONIO PADOA SCHIOPPA

Member
Professor Emeritus of Legal History at the University of Milan; former President of the Istituto Lombardo, Academy of Sciences and the Humanities, Milan; Corresponding Foreign Fellow of the Académie des inscriptions et belles-lettres, Institut de France, Paris

DOMINIQUE SCHNAPPER

Member
Research Director at the École des hautes études en sciences sociales (EHESS), Paris; Honorary Member of the French Conseil Constitutionnel

GOTTFRIED SCHOLZ   *Member*
Professor Emeritus of Music Analysis at the University of Music and Performing Arts, Vienna; Fellow of the Sudetendeutsche Akademie der Wissenschaften und Künste, Munich

MARJAN SCHWEGMAN   *Member*
Director of the Institute for War, Holocaust and Genocide Studies (NIOD), Royal Netherlands Academy of Arts and Sciences, Amsterdam; Professor of Political and Cultural History of the Twentieth Century, Utrecht University

QUENTIN SKINNER   *Member*
Barber Beaumont Professor of the Humanities, Queen Mary, University of London; Fellow of the British Academy and of Christ's College Cambridge; Foreign Fellow of the Accademia Nazionale dei Lincei, Rome

KARLHEINZ STIERLE   *Member*
Professor Emeritus of Romance Literature at the University of Constance; Member of the Heidelberger Akademie der Wissenschaften; Corresponding Fellow of the Académie des sciences morales et politiques, Institut de France, Paris; Foreign Fellow of the Accademia Nazionale dei Lincei, Rome

VICTOR STOICHITA   *Member*
Chair of Modern and Contemporary Art History at the University of Fribourg, Switzerland; Visiting Professor at the Istituto di studi italiani, University of Lugano; Foreign Fellow of the Accademia Nazionale dei Lincei, Rome

PETER SUTER   *Member*
Honorary Professor of Medicine at the University of Geneva; Former President of the Swiss Academies of Arts and Sciences

MARC VAN MONTAGU   *Member*
Professor Emeritus of Molecular Genetics at Ghent

University; Chairman of the Institute of Plant Bio-technology Outreach (IPBO), Ghent

CARLO WYSS

Member
Former Director for Accelerators at CERN. Expert in the design of superconducting acceleration cavities and magnets, for series manufacture by industry

SUZANNE WERDER

Secretary General

— 79 —

ber of the Paul Sacher Foundation; former Board Member of Pro Helvetia and former Member of the Swiss UNESCO committee

BALZAN PRIZEWINNERS
FOR LITERATURE, MORAL SCIENCES, AND THE ARTS, FOR PHYSICAL, MATHEMATICAL AND NATURAL SCIENCES, AND MEDICINE

(December 2013)

2013

ALAIN ASPECT (France) Quantum Information Processing and Communication
MANUEL CASTELLS (USA/Catalonia) Sociology
PASCALE COSSART (France) Infectious Diseases: basic and clinical aspects
ANDRÉ VAUCHEZ (France) Medieval History

2012

DAVID CHARLES BAULCOMBE (UK) Epigenetics
RONALD M. DWORKIN (USA) Jurisprudence
KURT LAMBECK (Australia/The Netherlands) Solid Earth Sciences, with emphasis on interdisciplinary research
REINHARD STROHM (UK/Germany) Musicology

2011

BRONISLAW BACZKO (Switzerland/Poland) Enlightenment Studies
PETER ROBERT LAMONT BROWN (USA/Ireland) Ancient History (The Graeco-Roman World)
RUSSELL SCOTT LANDE (UK/USA) Theoretical Biology or Bioinformatics
JOSEPH IVOR SILK (USA/UK) The Early Universe (From the Planck Time to the First Galaxies)

2010

MANFRED BRAUNECK (Germany) The History of Theatre in All Its Aspects
CARLO GINZBURG (Italy) European History (1400-1700)
JACOB PALIS (Brazil) Mathematics (pure and applied)
SHINYA YAMANAKA (Japan) Stem Cells: Biology and Potential Applications

2009

    TERENCE CAVE (UK) Literature since 1500

    MICHAEL GRÄTZEL (Switzerland/Germany) The Science of New Materials

    BRENDA MILNER (Canada/UK) Cognitive Neurosciences

    PAOLO ROSSI MONTI (Italy) History of Science

2008

    WALLACE S. BROECKER (USA) The Science of Climate Change

    MAURIZIO CALVESI (Italy) The Visual Arts since 1700

    IAN H. FRAZER (Australia/UK) Preventive Medicine

    THOMAS NAGEL (USA/Serbia) Moral Philosophy

2007

    ROSALYN HIGGINS (UK) International Law since 1945

    SUMIO IIJIMA (Japan) Nanoscience

    MICHEL ZINK (France) European Literature (1000-1500)

    BRUCE BEUTLER (USA) and JULES HOFFMANN (France/Luxembourg) Innate
        Immunity

2006

    LUDWIG FINSCHER (Germany) History of Western Music since 1600

    QUENTIN SKINNER (UK) Political Thought; History and Theory

    PAOLO DE BERNARDIS (Italy) and ANDREW LANGE (USA) Observational
        Astronomy and Astrophysics

    ELLIOT MEYEROWITZ (USA) and CHRISTOPHER SOMERVILLE (USA/Canada)
        Plant Molecular Genetics

2005

    PETER HALL (UK) The Social and Cultural History of Cities since the
        Beginning of the 16th Century

    LOTHAR LEDDEROSE (Germany) The History of the Art of Asia

    PETER and ROSEMARY GRANT (USA/UK) Population Biology

    RUSSELL HEMLEY (USA) and HO-KWANG MAO (USA/China) Mineral Physics

2004

    PIERRE DELIGNE (USA/Belgium) Mathematics

    NIKKI RAGOZIN KEDDIE (USA) The Islamic World from the End of the 19th
        to the End of the 20th Century

    MICHAEL MARMOT (UK) Epidemiology

    COLIN RENFREW (UK) Prehistoric Archaeology

2003

    REINHARD GENZEL (Germany) Infrared Astronomy
    ERIC HOBSBAWM (UK/Egypt) European History since 1900
    WEN-HSIUNG LI (USA/Taiwan) Genetics and Evolution
    SERGE MOSCOVICI (France/Romania) Social Psychology

2002

    WALTER JAKOB GEHRING (Switzerland) Developmental Biology
    ANTHONY THOMAS GRAFTON (USA) History of the Humanities
    XAVIER LE PICHON (France/Vietnam) Geology
    DOMINIQUE SCHNAPPER (France) Sociology

2001

    JAMES SLOSS ACKERMAN (USA) History of Architecture
    JEAN-PIERRE CHANGEUX (France) Cognitive Neurosciences
    MARC FUMAROLI (France) Literary History and Criticism (post 1500)
    CLAUDE LORIUS (France) Climatology

2000

    ILKKA HANSKI (Finland) Ecological Sciences
    MICHEL MAYOR (Switzerland) Instrumentation and Techniques in Astronomy
        and Astrophysics
    MICHAEL STOLLEIS (Germany) Legal History since 1500
    MARTIN LITCHFIELD WEST (UK) Classical Antiquity

1999

    LUIGI LUCA CAVALLI-SFORZA (USA/Italy) The Science of Human Origins
    JOHN ELLIOTT (UK) History, 1500-1800
    MIKHAEL GROMOV (France/Russia) Mathematics
    PAUL RICŒUR (France) Philosophy

1998

    HARMON CRAIG (USA) Geochemistry
    ROBERT MCCREDIE MAY (UK/Australia) Biodiversity
    ANDRZEJ WALICKI (USA/Poland) The Cultural and Social History of the
        Slavonic World

1997

    CHARLES COULSTON GILLISPIE (USA) History and Philosophy of Science
    THOMAS WILSON MEADE (UK) Epidemiology
    STANLEY JEYARAJA TAMBIAH (USA/Sri Lanka) Social Sciences: Social
        Anthropology

1996

    ARNO BORST (Germany) History: Medieval Cultures

    ARNT ELIASSEN (Norway) Meteorology

    STANLEY HOFFMANN (France/USA/Austria) Political Science: Contemporary
        International Relations

1995

    YVES BONNEFOY (France) Art History and Art Criticism

    CARLO M. CIPOLLA (Italy) Economic History

    ALAN J. HEEGER (USA) The Science of New Non-Biological Materials

1994

    NORBERTO BOBBIO (Italy) Law and Political Science

    RENÉ COUTEAUX (France) Biology

    FRED HOYLE (UK) and MARTIN SCHWARZSCHILD (USA/Germany) Astrophysics

1993

    WOLFGANG H. BERGER (USA/Germany) Palaeontology with special reference
        to Oceanography

    LOTHAR GALL (Germany) History: Societies of the 19th and 20th Centuries

    JEAN LECLANT (France) Art and Archaeology of the Ancient World

1992

    ARMAND BOREL (USA/Switzerland) Mathematics

    GIOVANNI MACCHIA (Italy) History and Criticism of Literature

    EBRAHIM M. SAMBA (Gambia) Preventive Medicine

1991

    GYÖRGY LIGETI (Austria/Hungary/Romania) Music

    VITORINO MAGALHÃES GODINHO (Portugal) History: The Emergence of
        Europe in the 15th and 16th Centuries

    JOHN MAYNARD SMITH (UK) Genetics and Evolution

1990

    WALTER BURKERT (Switzerland/Germany) The Study of the Ancient World

    JAMES FREEMAN GILBERT (USA) Geophysics

    PIERRE LALIVE D'EPINAY (Switzerland) Private International Law

1989

    EMMANUEL LÉVINAS (France/Lithuania) Philosophy

    LEO PARDI (Italy) Ethology

    MARTIN JOHN REES (UK) High Energy Astrophysics

1988
   SHMUEL NOAH EISENSTADT (Israel/Poland) Sociology
   RENÉ ÉTIEMBLE (France) Comparative Literature
   MICHAEL EVENARI (Israel/France) and OTTO LUDWIG LANGE (Germany)
      Applied Botany

1987
   JEROME SEYMOUR BRUNER (USA) Human Psychology
   RICHARD W. SOUTHERN (UK) Medieval History
   PHILLIP V. TOBIAS (South Africa) Physical Anthropology

1986
   OTTO NEUGEBAUER (USA/Austria) History of Science
   ROGER REVELLE (USA) Oceanography/Climatology
   JEAN RIVERO (France) Basic Human Rights

1985
   ERNST H.J. GOMBRICH (UK/Austria) History of Western Art
   JEAN-PIERRE SERRE (France) Mathematics

1984
   JAN HENDRIK OORT (The Netherlands) Astrophysics
   JEAN STAROBINSKI (Switzerland) History and Criticism of Literature
   SEWALL WRIGHT (USA) Genetics

1983
   FRANCESCO GABRIELI (Italy) Oriental Studies
   ERNST MAYR (USA/Germany) Zoology
   EDWARD SHILS (USA) Sociology

1982
   JEAN-BAPTISTE DUROSELLE (France) Social Sciences
   MASSIMO PALLOTTINO (Italy) Studies of Antiquity
   KENNETH VIVIAN THIMANN (USA/UK) Pure and Applied Botany

1981
   JOSEF PIEPER (Germany) Philosophy
   PAUL REUTER (France) International Public Law
   DAN PETER MCKENZIE, DRUMMOND HOYLE MATTHEWS and FREDERICK JOHN
      VINE (UK) Geology and Geophysics

1980
   ENRICO BOMBIERI (USA/Italy) Mathematics

Jorge Luis Borges (Argentina) Philology, Linguistics and Literary Criticism
Hassan Fathy (Egypt) Architecture and Urban Planning

1979

Torbjörn Caspersson (Sweden) Biology
Jean Piaget (Switzerland) Social and Political Science
Ernest Labrousse (France) and Giuseppe Tucci (Italy) History

1962

Paul Hindemith (Germany) Music
Andrej Kolmogorov (Russia) Mathematics
Samuel Eliot Morison (USA) History
Karl von Frisch (Austria) Biology

BALZAN PRIZEWINNERS
FOR HUMANITY, PEACE AND FRATERNITY
AMONG PEOPLES

2007   Karlheinz Böhm (Austria/Germany), Organisation *Menschen für Menschen*, Aid for Ethiopia

2004   Community of Sant'Egidio, DREAM programme combating AIDS and malnutrition in Mozambique

2000   Abdul Sattar Edhi (Pakistan/India)

1996   International Committee of the Red Cross, endeavours in the hospitals of Wazir Akbar Khan and Karte Seh in Kabul, Afghanistan

1991   Abbé Pierre (France)

1986   United Nations Refugee Agency

1978   Mother Teresa of Calcutta (India/Macedonia)

1962   H.H. John XXIII (Vatican City/Italy)

1961   Nobel Foundation

FINITO DI STAMPARE
PER CONTO DI LEO S. OLSCHKI EDITORE
PRESSO ABC TIPOGRAFIA • SESTO FIORENTINO (FI)
NEL MESE DI SETTEMBRE 2014

THE ANNUAL BALZAN LECTURE

1. *The Evolution of Darwin's Finches, Mockingbirds and Flies*, by Peter and Rosemary Grant. 2010.

2. *Humanists with Inky Fingers. The Culture of Correction in Renaissance Europe*, by Anthony Thomas Grafton. 2011.

3. *Cognitive Archaeology from Theory to Practice: the Early Cycladic Sanctuary at Keros*, by Colin Renfrew. 2012.

4. *Fair Society, Healthy Lives*, by Michael Marmot. 2013.

5. *Of Moon and Land, Ice and Strand: Sea Level during Glacial Cycles*, by Kurt Lambeck. 2014.